Pandemonium

VAG ABO NDS

Series editor: Max Haiven

Also available

001

Pandemonium

Proliferating Borders of Capital
and the Pandemic Swerve

Angela Mitropoulos

PLUTO PRESS

First published 2020 by Pluto Press
345 Archway Road, London N6 5AA

www.plutobooks.com

British Library Cataloguing in Publication Data
A catalogue record for this book is available from the
British Library

ISBN   978 0 7453 4330 3   Paperback
ISBN   978 0 7453 4331 0   PDF eBook
ISBN   978 0 7453 4322 8   Kindle eBook
ISBN   978 0 7453 4321 1   EPUB eBook

This book is printed on paper suitable for recycling
and made from fully managed and sustained forest
sources. Logging, pulping and manufacturing processes
are expected to conform to the environmental
standards of the country of origin.

Typeset by Stanford DTP Services, Northampton,
England

Simultaneously printed in the United Kingdom and
United States of America

VĀG
ABO
NDS

Contents

VAG
ABO
NDS

Acknowledgments

Many thanks go to Max Haiven and all those at VAGABONDS and Pluto Press who worked through difficult times, to Matt Kiem, S.L. Lim, Thomas Lynch, Wenny Theresia, Liz Thompson, Sanmati Verma, Liz Crash, *New Inquiry*, Out of the Woods, *New Socialist*, *Transversal* and, not least, the reviewers who patiently read through early versions. Caveats concerning blame for any shortcomings apply. May the churn build a new world.

Introduction

How we make sense of the pandemic is based on assumptions about the origins of the virus, the causes of disease and death with which it is associated, and contested views regarding what it exposed or revealed or is known. Understandings of disorder, like perceptions of chaos, or definitions of crisis and threat, depend a great deal on perspective and assumptions of what an orderly world might otherwise be. John Milton coined 'Pandæmonium' for his epic, mid-seventeenth-century poem *Paradise Lost*. It means 'all demons'—from the Greek '*pan*' for 'all.' His use marked a shift from the meaning of '*daemon*' as ministering oracle to that of fallen angel or malign supernatural being. In *Paradise Lost*, Pandæmonium is the name of the capital city of Hell—an infernal gathering on the shore of the Lake of Fire, where disobedient angels deliberate on whether there is hope of regaining heaven or whether to believe in ancient prophecies of a new creation. Here, 'pandemonium' instead describes the emergence of an order from treatments of chaos—and it does so without the nostalgic assumption that what went before the pandemic was a paradise undone by disobedience and sin. How and whether the pandemic presents a turning-point or swerve, and toward what, is the question to which this book is addressed.

In terms of scale, the microbial event of a new virus will arguably come to represent the largest intensive swerve of the first quarter of the twenty-first century. By the end of April 2020, New York City hospital mortuaries, crematories, and city-run morgues had run out of space. Some were resorting to refrigerated trailers. More than 17,000 people had died from the disease—almost five times more than died in the Twin Towers on September 11, 2001.

A swerve, or *clinamen*, was how the ancient Roman poet Lucretius described the cascading effects from one molecular movement in his epic poem *On the Nature of Things*—and in his deliberations on the plague that accompanied the fall of Athenian empire. There, he offers a theory of natural causes at odds with the major traditions in so-called Western philosophy which holds that it is within the nature of things to realize a destiny that was present at their origins and according to their rank. Lucretian philosophy points elsewhere. It refutes the subordination of lives to the assumptions of an idealized Way of Life and, by setting aside the sorting between unruly matter and eternal forms on which that idealization depends, the unaccountable, transcendent fatalism implicit in the terminology of the natural disaster. But if the precise, contingent base point from which a swerve happens cannot be known in advance— the molecular change in the protein spike that sets SARS-CoV-2 apart from other coronaviruses and which, among the numerous mutations for which viruses have a remarkable capacity, managed to survive repeated encounters with human immune systems—both responses to the pandemic and the conditions of human health have been centuries in the making.

Some of those responses have drawn on understandings of health and disease that are models of social order recast as an eternal nature, rendering those responses ineffective in stemming the transmission of disease. Despite drawing on the analogy of contagion to redescribe crises, much the same is true of the risk analyst Nassim Taleb's black swan, in which the question becomes how to convert an unforeseeable event and spreading crisis into an opportunity for financial gain. The black swan is simply the name for a programmable response to uncertainty that treats nonlinear effects as if they were a universal repeating pattern found in nature. These approaches redefine what an effective response to a pandemic means. Bluntly, while some responses have been turned toward saving lives, others have sought to enhance and preserve the very system that has conditioned the patterning of illness and deaths. As with the biosecurity and disaster apparatus elaborated after 9/11, definitions of threat and security, however implicit, can convene and justify actions that multiply death and suffering along certain lines.

The title of this book is also a gesture to Michel Foucault's *The Order of Things*—the English title of the work in which he presents his theory of how the production of knowledge is always a matter of power relations. It points, moreover, to debates and assumptions concerning neoliberalism.

Against the conventional view of neoliberalism, not only did borders proliferate, but they did so largely without challenging the assumption that they are a means of protection against the ravages of capitalist exploitation rather than the arbitrage which makes exploitation possible. This facilitated the turn between neoliberal government and the resurgence of the far Right.[1]

This is not to suggest that the approach taken here follows Foucault—except in foregrounding these debates and the epistemological question of how we know what we know, or think we know.[2] More so, it is to point out that *The Order of Things* is an allusion to the eighteenth-century political economist Adam Smith's repeated turn of phrase: "the natural course and order of things." In Smith's economic liberalism, that presumably natural economic order could not be realized through sovereign rule but, instead, would be providentially manifested by the self-interest of property-owners, whose decisions would be guided by knowledge of the "wealth of nations." This is the figure of *homo economicus*, or 'rational economic man.' The invisible hand is revealed to economic man, in other words, by the Gross Domestic Product (GDP)—a metric that Smith envisaged but that did not quite emerge until the twentieth century. For Smith's contemporary, the reactionary cleric and political-economist Thomas Malthus, the natural economic order could only be revealed by eliminating the moral hazard of parish welfare. For him, the price of bread would be the spur to individual moral-economic decisions. The misery that ensued as the result of the withdrawal of welfare would serve as a proxy for the biblical plagues and famines by re-enacting a purportedly natural means of death for large segments of the 'unproductive' population. Much has been made of the contrast between these crucial thinkers whose prolonged influence cannot be overstated, irrespective of whether they are still read. Yet these prototypical approaches to economic liberalism and authoritarian government are both premised on the idea of the household (*oikos*) as the primordial economic unit and presumably natural justification of exploitation. Put simply, they were both moral economists from whom the idealized (patriarchal) household served as the model of a proper law and order.

Briefly, the idea of a natural economic hierarchy is the assumption, derived from medieval estates and ancient texts on household management, of a heritable patriarchal authority over women, children and, not least, bonded servants and bound slaves. It is the source of contemporary (mis)understandings of gender and race and, in their abstraction from the history of the feudal estates and plantation economies from which capitalism emerged, their disconnection from distinct understandings of class. The false choice between liberal and reactionary forms of economic management premised on the hierarchical household (*oikos*)—and its indivisible personification in a politics from which its subordinates are excluded—has become the model for almost all systems of modern political authoritarianism and economic liberalism. Because it naturalizes the asymmetries of surplus-value extraction, it is not outside the circuit of capital but integral to its systems of accumulation, particularly in moments of that circuit's crises.[3]

Understanding this systematic logic helps in theorizing the politics of the pandemic in a way that highlights the centrality of the economic unit of 'the household'—as well as the infrastructures and supply chains of healthcare, communication and food without which no private household could survive the lockdown. It also makes it possible to see how stay-at-home orders have not made the lives of those trapped with abusers or those without affordable or any housing safer, even as in other instances it has amplified the outsourcing of gendered conflicts over household work to domestic service and supply workers— and to link the entitlements that foster intimate violence to those of macroeconomic policy and geopolitics. As, for instance, in the discussions of epidemiological mathematics and money below suggests, the practices of statistical knowledge and workings of national currencies are pivotal to the naturalization and extraction of surplus value. These overlapping practices of governance, no less than overt articulations of racism, ableism or sexism, point to neoliberalism's endogenous turning-points to authoritarian and fascist politics. At the same time, this book presents a warning against treating economic liberalism and economic nationalism as fundamentally irreconcilable—particularly when the crisis to which solutions are addressed is that of capitalism rather than health.

Moreover, the appearance of the virus in China in late 2019 and its later spread to 'the West' makes it important to address the idea of a natural economy in its national and geopolitical scales, even where 'natural economy' is rendered as an anthropological aesthetics of cultural differences and units. Chief among these is the return of the East-West dichotomy and insinuations of Eastern uniformity. As comparisons of epidemiological curves suggest however, the dichotomy is an imaginative orientalist fiction. Singapore, the Philippines and Bangladesh had comparable peaks to those of Sweden, Hungary, the United Kingdom and the United States. Malaysia's arc was similar to the Netherlands. The peaks and falls in Thailand, China, Taiwan and Vietnam approximated those of New Zealand, Norway and Austria. While this does not describe the uneven conditions within each of those countries, it nevertheless illustrates the absence of generic Eastern or Western approaches and experiences.

Despite this, for some the global pandemic prompted a return to discredited imperialist maps of geocultural uniformity and division. In one increasingly popular rendition there is a nostalgia for a "deep structure" of Western philosophy's ancient categorical teleology that is said to give rise to a necessary law and order. Having regrettably been lost in the West, it is fortuitously rediscoverable in the East's "Confucian ways of thinking" and its presumably unique respect for professional expertise and "hyper-sensitivity to disorder."[4] Informed by Kantian geopolitical anthropology (the source of the idea of distinct 'continental' races), and nurturing a Machiavellian preoccupation with having the ear of aspiring princes, the ascription of cultural uniformity is an attempt to circumscribe class conflict to an implicitly ethnonationalist orbit of geocultural 'self-regulation' or discipline.

This is how the recent history of conflicts over healthcare, pensions and work in China that preceded and shaped the impact of the disease have been erased, including by much of the Anglophone and European left. For instance, there is little discussion of the ways in which China's *hukou* or household welfare registration system fostered the geographic (and often gendered) inequalities in which coastal cities were privileged, as compared to inland cities such as Wuhan, the privatization and commercialization of its healthcare system, or the waves of strikes throughout China over the years that might shake the idea of a unique cultural bond between governments and populations.[5]

Yet geoculturalism is also a diagram that, in seeking to derive a law and order from imputed anthropological variations, converges with far-right ethnopluralism—such as that promoted in the 1960s and '70s by Alain de Benoist and France's *Nouvelle Droite*. It is an important ideological inspiration of today's global far-right insurgency—particularly those who insist they are not white supremacists but, merely, adherents of the idea of unique ethnological or cultural differences which must be preserved through global segregation. Simply because they draw on seventeenth-century European anthropological and cultural understandings of race—as distinct from more recent biological or 'scientific' concepts of race—does not mean that geocultural paradigms are any less concerned than seventeenth-century European colonists and powers with using race as the predicate of law and order and the justification for an associated imperial cartography.

In their preoccupation with the geopolitics of race, order and chaos, these thinkers are far from alone. Speculation about the post-Covid world and the new world borders it is shaping are informed by perceptions of chaos that are manipulated into the seemingly self-evident intuition for a new geopolitical order. That geopolitical order assumes a modular system of economic nationalism that draws on ethnopluralism.

The stakes, however, concern the very logic of capital, which requires the assignment and enforcement of well-defined property rights so as to proceed through and conclude its asymmetric, exploitative circuit. The actual system to which this gives rise is far more archipelagic in its spatial and temporal arrangements than diagrams of global nationalism assert. It is turned to creating groups of workers and populations placed outside citizenship or the full scope of political and economic rights.[6] Contrary to the economic nationalist idea of self-sufficient (re)production, all borders have always been porous. Accumulation involves filtering, not a fixed impermeable line. In practice, then, geocultural approaches simply convert the logic of capital, through the repertoire of cultural aesthetics, into a global political predicate of capitalist lawmaking exclusive of large swathes of workers. In treating culture as an inherited and unique property, cultural nationalism, economic nationalism and geocultural approaches implicitly treat nations and economic management as analogous to an idealized familial and patriarchal household. From that point on, they mystify the quest to install a boundary between 'proper' political representation of the nation and a purportedly 'proper' economic policy which regulates the movement of workers. In the orientalist version promulgated during the pandemic, the 'lost' system of a classical ('Western') exclusion of slaves, women, and children from politics is simply projected onto and rediscovered in a generic, contemporary 'Asia' as its fortuitous manifestation.

On the other side of the Pacific, in what we are told is a world away, Donald Trump's seemingly chaotic rule in the US has involved a systematic effort to remove the political rights of large parts of the workforce (through disenfranchisement, limits on citizenship and the cudgel of detention and deportation). However frustrated or incompetent that effort has been, it has been consistent and consistently shaped his response to the pandemic. For all their differences, the Chinese and American governments' responses have been shaped by a similar logic. In the US case, the dream of a workforce stripped of political rights and relegated to economic subordination (the *oikos* in the classical formulation) has animated Trump as much as it has shaped the US administration's geopolitical affinity toward authoritarian government elsewhere.

All taxonomies involve a theory of origins and epistemology—which is where this book begins. Exotic explanations of the virus and the pandemic project a fixed, idealized version of economic, social and political arrangements onto nature. It is an idea of nature at odds with what is known of the virus or biological, microbial and evolutionary processes—including human evolution and biology. Much like exogenous theories of crisis, exoticist explanations of the virus and disease engage in a preliminary polemical and metaphysical division, and go on to advance an argument about the assignment and displacement of liabilities. During the pandemic, while much of the risk of the disease was displaced onto private households—and therefore the patterning of (heritable) assets and liquid wages—those households were linked through an assumed racial genealogy to larger (national and geopolitical) taxonomies of populations and the management of their health and welfare. However, the viability of locked-down households was physically contingent upon and linked by the unpaid and low-paid work in which women, migrants, and Black and Brown people predominate. The way in which these designated essential services routinely function is through low and below-subsistence wages. During the pandemic, they were maintained, then, by the lurking possibility of hunger and homelessness—against which workers had to weigh the chances of infection, in many cases in the absence of adequate protective equipment and healthcare.

As the final parts of this book go on to argue, elisions of these contingencies establish the preliminary steps and momentum of post-pandemic economic policy. That trajectory foreshadows a post-Malthusian argument and offer of a political-economic social contract, according to which the crises of national productivity (falls in the GDP, rising unemployment) wrought by lockdowns should be solved by the 'restoration' of boundaries that restores a growing rate of capital accumulation. This is by no means inevitable. Yet rather than render a vast and diverse opposition to and movements against that trajectory into an object, the approach here is concerned with highlighting the limits to that movement and the points on which force might be exerted so that there is, indeed, movement in another direction.

The second and third parts of this book discuss the quarantine and population theory. The seemingly self-evident retrieval of the quarantine from the medieval past and colonial margins figures prominently as a practice-run in merging authoritarian governance with private, selective healthcare. It suggests that the priority accorded to the language of quarantine—and the travel bans that encouraged a disingenuous conflation of quarantines with case isolation and therefore the geographic association of groups of people with a disease—cannot be explained as a consequence of the urgent need to stem the transmission of the virus since there is little evidence of quarantine's efficacy in this regard. Rather, the apparently spontaneous retrieval of the quarantine crystallized a decades-long, endogenous shift within neoliberalism.

What prevailing understandings of neoliberalism have obscured is the importance to capitalist extraction and accumulation of a political-economic boundary between the *demos* (the ostensibly proper subject of political representation and lawmaking) and the practices of managing (properly) productive populations.

The third part of the book traces the history of "herd immunity" through the history of population theory. It highlights the importance of a boundary between the economic concept of populations (whose value is defined and measured in terms of production and reproduction) and the political idea of a *demos* (the boundary of the political contract). This history is linked to the emergence of the national welfare state and the epidemiological statistical reformulation of a Malthusian constraint or 'natural limits' which abstractly encoded racial and immigration restrictions and justified limits on healthcare expenditure. In doing so, it underlines the varied influences of cultural nationalism and early fascism on statistical knowledge and understandings of population health and eugenics—and contrasts these with Marx's understanding of class.

The fourth part begins with the first political philosopher of eugenics, Plato—for whom prescribed drugs were both a eugenic instrument and a metaphor for acceptably mendacious political speech. The principal focus, here, is on the promotion of hydroxychloroquine as an attempt to circumvent the clinical trial and restrictions on drug prescription and advertising. It suggests that the two key uncertainties in pharmacological capital are those of the drug trial and the sale of the product (the creation of a growing market). Yet it also underscores the importance of the Platonist exemption for intuitive, patriarchal knowledge to the history of philosophical rationalism, of charismatic or entrepreneurial uncertainty during a perceived time of political disorder, and in overcoming key obstacles to the ordered realization of the capitalist circuit.

The fifth section begins with a discussion of the collapse of GDP during the pandemic, and goes on to focus on financial and insurance instruments and supply-chains. Specifically, it takes up the World Bank's pandemic bond and the logistics of personal protective equipment (PPE) supply. The pandemic bond points to a financialization of the imagination of disaster, as do all catastrophe bonds. When compared with another relevant catastrophe bond (the extreme mortality bond) issued by a reinsurer, however, the pandemic bond more clearly represents the transformation of intergovernmental disaster aid to cash-strapped governments into the effective purchase of insurance on capital markets by the bond's sponsoring governments (Australia, Germany and Japan). It preserved austerity as regular policy. Moreover, the stipulations of the pandemic bond froze the supply of money at the moment in which it would have been most effective in stemming disease transmission.

While the cash was destined to pay for PPE, global private markets for PPE were being reshaped by public-private consortia working in tandem to monopolize lucrative supply-lines and those markets. This suggests that the collapse of the pandemic preparedness policies of, for instance, previous US administrations was less a problem of which politicians were in power than the securitization of disaster and the commercialization of health and disease. On the one hand, those policies were highly amenable to a merger of insurance with financial speculation—as with catastrophe bonds. On the other, manufacturers had scaled back on production of devices because they did not think that the products would find a market. The problem is less the absence of preparation or just-in-time systems than that preventative and life-saving equipment is a commodity. In that regard, the claims of economic nationalism around PPE supply-chains has far less to do with ensuring that needs are met than with mercantilism and facilitating the monopolistic carving-up of global markets through the combined action of states and corporations. At the same time, the involvement of corporations such as DuPont illustrates the indistinction of states and markets and, moreover, the highly contradictory positions that corporations can hold in relation to health because each of those positions is a financial measure of risk that can be hedged (or insured against).

The final section looks forward to the terms of post-Covid-19 policy. The overly-familiar mechanisms of resolving a defined crisis in national productivity are summarized as austerity. They include a contraction of wages and social incomes so as to increase profit margins as well as the elaboration of authoritarian governance over populations. The current include immigration restrictions, which make labour market arbitrage possible and furnish a reservoir of hyper-exploitation, and the expansion of surveillance, which accomplishes much the same thing. Yet the current circumstances present this familiar scenario with a dilemma. Malthus had sought to characterize poverty and unemployment as a function of 'overpopulation.' Those characterizations are not immediately available in circumstances of a declining population, rises in unemployment as a result of lockdowns (not migration) and the preponderance of migrant workers in what, during the pandemic, had been designated as critical infrastructure. Nevertheless, the gathering momentum is toward a reckoning of (national economic) debts owed in the form of surplus labor—presented as heroic sacrifice, justified as the presumably natural thresholds of political and economic rights. Not least, it is made possible by the selective prohibitions on mourning that desensitizes against a eugenic trimming of the 'unproductive' or 'surplus' populations.

At the same time however, the pandemic also presents us with another understanding of debt as an acknowledgment of the interdependent conditions of survival and care. It is a moment in which what it takes to live, to be healthy and flourish, vividly clashes with the capitalist mystique of economic productivity, of the idealized household and the metrics of the Gross National Product.

Origin of the Species

In late December 2019, doctors in Wuhan, China began reporting acute cases of pneumonia caused by an unknown microbial agent for which there was no known course of treatments. By April 22 2020, there were some 2.6 million confirmed cases of infection around the world, around 184,000 deaths attributed to the disease, and much of the world was in a partial lockdown in an effort to stem its transmission.

Beyond this barest description, most explanations put forward a theory of origins linked to a distinctive epistemology, or how we know what we know, or think we do. On April 22, Trump described the virus as the "Invisible Enemy" while announcing an almost-complete prohibition on immigration, including preventing most people currently outside of the US from becoming permanent residents—presumably to strengthen the implication that it is a foreign virus, and having withdrawn federal funding for the testing that would make the virus visible. The sweeping immigration decree was announced at the very moment when there were some 845,822 confirmed cases of infection and 47,479 deaths in the US—the highest in the world at the time.

Strenuous debates animate nearly all aspects of how we understand this disease, from explanations of the origins of the virus to the accounting of deaths. One review from eleven countries suggested that there were around 28,000 unaccounted-for deaths in April 2020 that had not been attributed to the pandemic, but that would be difficult to account for otherwise.[7] By mid-April, it became apparent that while there had been outbreaks in around 18 percent of aged care facilities across the UK (some 2,000), the number of deaths attributed to Covid-19 in the official toll only took into account those who had died in hospitals, not deaths in either care homes or elsewhere. Moreover, as Reuters reported, based on documents in the UK, hospital admission protocols and the pressure to move non-acute patients from wards (including back to aged care homes with less access to protective equipment), may have had a significant impact on the number of deaths and led to inaccurate figures.[8]

The reasons for discrepancies in figures may not be nefarious in each instance or in whole. Nevertheless, much hangs on their accuracy, and there are vast implications either way—including how lives are valued and their loss mourned. Evaluation is never innocent. Some of those accounting practices stem from the calculations of life and accident insurance, through which the measure of a worthy life amounts to a reckoning that occurs at the moment of death or injury, but in its classical sense understood as the interruption or cessation of a productive life.[9] As we shall see, a measure of productivity (GDP) was incorporated into the structuring of the World Bank's pandemic bond, but not a related catastrophe bond that furnished liquidity within the insurance industry and a hedge for pension fund investors. More broadly, definitions of the value of a life lost according to (distinctly capitalist) measures and definitions of productivity has been foregrounded in demands to 'reopen the economy'. These have included weighing the risks—including the potential political risks—of a break with austerity, notably balancing the potential impact of partial economic shutdowns on the GDP against the likelihood of an increase in illness and death of business as usual.

Origins

Wuhan, the capital of Hubei province, is an inland port city of some 11 million people. Established by trading posts on the Yangtze River, it is currently a major international logistics hub and massive engine of exploitation. Shaped by fossil-fueled, state-run industrialization from the 1950s to the 1970s, it has been transformed, as other cities in China have, by one of the most rapid and largest rural-to-urban migrations in recent history, economic restructuring and privatization. In Wuhan, this economic restructuring has been a joint state-corporate venture, marked not least by the privatization of healthcare and public housing throughout the 1980s and 1990s. Patterns of welfare and housing subsidy (the *hukou*) have yielded vast disparities between urban- and migrant-classed households.[10]

Today, Wuhan is defined by steel foundries, concrete and other construction-related industries, car manufacturing plants, post-industrial trade and research precincts, and global corporate brands, such as the Dongfeng Peugeot Citroen Automobile factory. As *Chuǎng* point out, Wuhan is "dotted by the slowly-cooling blast furnaces of the remnant state-owned iron and steel foundries." It is also known as one of the "four furnaces"—cities in China which experience oppressively hot and humid summers.[11] It has recorded some of the worst sustained levels of air pollution of any city in the world.[12] China's decentralized, commercially-oriented health system and the lack of healthcare coverage did, in all likelihood, worsen the impact of Covid-19. In 2007, most of the 140 million workers in China's informal economy did not have access to health insurance. Some argue these circumstances already had an immense impact during the first SARS outbreak in 2002.[13] In this context, the recent high-profile rapid construction of dedicated Covid-19 hospitals quite possibly represents an effort by parts of government to expand healthcare and insurance coverage—albeit under the administrative control of the military.

At the same time, while the response to the first SARS outbreak targeted internal migrants, the response by the Chinese government to Covid-19 in 2020 was largely organized through lockdowns and systems of household, neighborhood and technological surveillance. It is part of the evolution of a system, in which populations that have been actively created as precarious by decades of economic policy can now only access what should be routine health care by volunteering for experimental emergency procedures. This may or may not have increased their chances of recovery, but they bear many of the downside risks of any possible (presumably eventual patented) vaccine, as well as other drug and biotechnical developments. Notably, the collapse of public healthcare in China was accompanied by the introduction of a system in which hospital administrators were permitted "to profit-earn from new pharmaceuticals and medical technologies (after strong lobbying by the relevant multinational corporations), with salary bonuses for the staff involved."[14]

These were the circumstances in which SARS-CoV-2 appeared, and according to which the severity of Covid-19 was undoubtedly worsened by the prevalence and patterns of chronic illnesses stemming from pollution, economic exploitation and lack of care. This was indicated very early by the strong link between pre-existing conditions and the severity of pneumonia and cardiovascular diseases associated with the virus.

Yet in China and elsewhere, these larger stories about the systemic and structural conditions of the course of disease have disappeared. Reductive accounts of disease causality tend to be demanded by private insurance as it reckons its own liabilities and attempts to displace them, often onto the alleged failings of individuals. Other times, susceptibility to illness is reduced to a racist taxonomy where groups are held to be 'at risk' of ailments (notably diabetes, hypertension, or heart disease) yet the factors that rendered them as such are erased. It is an erasure that tacitly endorses claims of an intrinsic (biological) inferiority and, perhaps because those conditions are far from unique to Wuhan, in discussions of the origins of the virus.

What is remarkable about many of these origin stories of the virus is how much emphasis has been accorded to seemingly exotic explanations, notably Wuhan's wet markets and purportedly culturally-unique dietary habits. These were joined in the popular (and often racist) imagination by exotic interpretations of mundane events such as microbial species-jumping, or the similarly exotic but more explicit science fiction of a virus made in a laboratory, perhaps as a bioweapon. Less salacious but no less orientalist, other commentators opined that the disease's origins lay in a social and institutional context dominated by 'Asian values' of deference, opacity and atavistic tradition that allegedly prevented scientists, bureaucrats and others from taking effective action in time to stop the spread.

Initial attempts to downplay the seriousness of the virus have not been unique to China either. Of course, the virus had, at the very least, existed two weeks prior to doctors' reporting of patients with acute and untreatable pneumonia in Wuhan's hospitals. It existed before its genetic sequencing and identification as a novel coronavirus. Authorities in China had, for a time, tried to subdue reports of a novel, severe and highly-infectious disease—as indeed did other governments, including the Trump administration and the recently re-elected UK Conservative government in their public insistence that they were prepared and everything was under control. Both the Chinese and US governments treated whistle-blowers as a threat during important moments in the course of the pandemic. Moreover, the lurch from secrecy to complacency to lockdowns in all these cases did not always follow the line of known evidence about what might effectively stem the transmission of a contagious disease. Where evidence-based decision-making did occur, it was largely the result of sustained public pressure on governments from healthworkers, epidemiologists, researchers and, indeed, those for whom the lives of people in China are as important as the lives of people anywhere else.

Taxonomy

Despite their outward variety, every exoticist explanation of the pandemic shares the epistemic assumption of an ideal taxonomic order and its boundaries: a supposedly natural hierarchy of value, based on what are presumed to be biological facts. It is often accompanied by assumptions that health involves purity— despite what we know of immunity or human evolution. In such taxonomies, the virus and its destructive effects are explained as a consequence of that ideal order's disarray. By that logic, the disease becomes the implied evidence of a fallen world; its destructive impact, a possibly regrettable but necessary warning to return to that order. These assumptions link narratives about the origins of the virus with responses that are ineffective but appear to be self-evident because their goal is to restore an order that, in truth, has never existed as the narrative purports it should.

Claims that the virus was made in a laboratory are resonant (in spite of the absence of any evidence for such claims) in part because they assert belief in a boundary between culture and nature—more precisely: a dichotomy between human artifice and divinely-ordained nature derived from Natural Law theology. Like the Red Queen in the *Resident Evil* film franchise or similar cultural texts from at least *Frankenstein* on, it is a cautionary tale about what happens when humans usurp divine authority and mess with the natural order, even with the best of intentions. Unlike *Resident Evil*, those who insist on the lab-made virus theory are incapable of reflecting critically on their own genre—as does the movie franchise's final characterisation of its principal antagonist, a figure who comes to view death and human suffering as the workings of divine punishment and salvation.

The preoccupation of many with Wuhan's wet markets and bats may seem more plausible because it approximates a prominent phylogenetic hypothesis—albeit calibrated to induce a visceral reaction. Seemingly more science than fiction, it merely shifts the scene of cultivation, from that of a virus cultured in a laboratory to that of a virus brought about by the unclear/unclean boundaries of cultural and agricultural practices. To do so, it overlays the resonant nature/culture paradigm across an incomplete genetic and evolutionary map, fills in the unknowns and conditions of phylogenetic statements, and reads statistical probabilities as necessity. That is, geneticists have found that there is a closer than average genetic distance between SARS-CoV-2 and two coronaviruses that have been found in bats, namely RaTG13 and RmYN02. This does not mean that bats carry the SARS-CoV-2 virus. Nor that they passed along a mutated variety to humans. What it means is that, according to the available sampling of coronaviruses among mammals, bats have been identified as a likely but distant point in the evolutionary history of SARS-CoV-2.

Because bats have turned out to be a distant point in evolutionary time and phylogenetic space, the pangolin has been put forward as an intermediary host. For now, it is a theoretical missing link. So far, the connection to SARS-CoV-2 has not been established.[15] It may be that something becomes known of an unknown pangolin coronavirus in the meantime which strengthens the case for their being the intermediary. The absence of evidence, while serving as a prompt for further research and genome sequencing, does not however quite explain how the pangolin came to the forefront as a candidate once the bat fell through.

In her 1966 book *Purity and Danger*, the anthropologist Mary Douglas spent a remarkable amount of time discussing the pangolin—the "benign monster" that, in her account, the Lele, who lived near the Kasai River in Central Africa, sacrificed in "ritual homage" and then proceeded to eat. As Douglas put it: the pangolin "contradicts all the most obvious animal categories. It is scaly like a fish, but it climbs trees. It is more like an egg-laying lizard than a mammal, yet it suckles its young." The meanings that Douglas ascribed to the pangolin may not have been the same as the Lele. The ritual was, nevertheless, for Douglas, clearly a moment that "combines all the elements" she suggests are otherwise kept apart. It was undoubtedly an important inspiration for the book, serving as "a profound meditation on the nature of purity and impurity," a ritual that prompted her "to turn round and confront the categories ... and to recognise them for the fictive, man-made, arbitrary creations that they are." It is likely that it fascinated Douglas because it over-turned the categorical assumptions of taxonomy from which she—and anthropology—had barely emerged, including the idea of 'primitive cultures' as an early (or lower) stage of human develop-ment and (racial) cultural variation. Nevertheless, as Douglas points out, she was told little of the "cult songs," except one "tantalising line," which she translated as: "'Now I will enter the house of affliction,' [which] they sing as initiates carry its corpse round the village."[16]

Speciation

Douglas is not alone in having insisted that categor-ical differences between species are an "arbitrary creation." Indeed, the title of Darwin's *Origin of the Species* is arguably ironic in that it does not answer the question implied in the title. Rather, it treats evolution as a set of questions to be answered, which had previously been assumed to have been already answered by classical accounts of biological variation. For classical biology, each category and its participants are classed by their possession of a unique property, and origins are teleologically linked to ends by reference to that unique essence. Its most emphatic diagram is the *scala natura*—an eternal universe of fixed, hierarchical ranks that makes it possible to judge the fidelity of the material world to an imputed divine law. Darwin cut the teleological cord by insisting that usefulness was not intrinsic to any preserved trait but contingent on a changing environment—a point that is worth recalling in explanations of the origins of SARS-CoV-2, whose principal environment in this scenario is the conditions of human health. More so, Darwin suggested that "genera are merely artificial combinations made for convenience," since the essential property that distinguishes a species is "undiscoverable."[17]

As for the discoveries of microbiology, bioinformatics and genomics since Darwin, they have hastened the subordination of taxonomy (classification) to systematics (relationships). In doing so, they have illustrated a world in which viruses are one of the most abundant things on the planet, and in which zoonosis (the transmission of microbes from one species to another) is not always pathogenic and often mundane. Indeed, humans are more likely than not to be the evolutionary result of the zoonotic, recombinant action of bacterial genetics transmitted through viral infections.[18] In contrast to a classical obsession with rigid categories, hierarchies and taxonomies of life, recent science has stressed a complex interdependence.

When Lynn Margulis outlined her ground-breaking argument for the importance of symbiosis in evolution in 1971, she began by suggesting that "every living thing belongs primarily to one or another of two groups that are mutually exclusive: organisms with cells that have nuclei [eukaryotes] and organisms with cells that do not [prokaryotes]" The "exception" to this distinction, she added in parentheses, "is viruses and virus-like particles, but such organisms can reproduce only inside cells."[19] Research since then has confirmed viruses' capacity to render that mutually-exclusive distinction obsolete: viruses are metabolically-inert outside of cells but, inside cells, capable of being rather sophisticated mechanisms of genetic transfer and therefore creative of complex, overlapping genetic histories.

Deleuze and Guattari would describe this as the moment in which Darwin's tree of life, each with its distinct and isolatable branch, gives way to the microbial rhizome in the history and philosophy of the natural sciences. "We evolve and die," Deleuze and Guattari insisted, "more from our polymorphous and rhizomatic flus than from hereditary diseases, or diseases that have their own line of descent."[20] But if, as they go on to add, the "rhizome is an anti-genealogy," that cannot be said of the ways in which genealogy is seemingly affirmed by patterns of exposure, ill-health, exploitation and inherited wealth. The arboreal metaphor was certainly given a distinctly Malthusian emphasis in 'social Darwinism.' A segregationist impulse was certainly fortified by the so-called Modern Evolutionary Synthesis, which merged population genetics with Ernst Mayr's iso-lationist concept of speciation in the 1930s and '40s. Yet Darwin himself regarded the tree as a rough, heuristic metaphor.

Indeed Marx's eager response to the publica-tion of Darwin's *On the Origin of Species* in 1859 suggests the genealogical tree was not the book's groundbreaking, scandalous import. Months after its publication, Marx wrote that it was "most important and suits my purpose in that it provides a basis in natural science for the historical class struggle." "For the first time," Marx enthused, "'teleology' in natural science is not only dealt a mortal blow but its rational meaning is empir-ically explained." In the 1888 preface to the *Communist Manifesto*, Engels recommends the text to readers by claiming that his and Marx's theory of class struggle is "destined to do for history what Darwin's theory has done for biology," which "we both of us, had been gradually approaching for some years before [they met in] 1845."[21] For Marx, Darwin's contribution was to show that biology, nature and ecology are no more governed by teleology than culture, history or economics — any more than catastrophes of the environment can be invested with an eschatological or provi-dential significance.

Herding

As for the concept of population: throughout his writings, Marx describes a shift from the genea-logical inscriptions of feudal property rights—in which "[b]irth determines the quality of the monarch [much] as it determines the quality of cattle"—to its capitalist reinscriptions. The latter gives rise, on the one hand, to an individuation that "makes the herd-like existence superfluous and dissolves it" into an idealized community of proprietors and, on the other, furnishes a system of exchange that the "worker tries to make a meal of, and which makes a meal of him" instead.[22] The distinction Marx is alluding to is a classical theme of inherited (property) rights and man's dominion over things and nature. Articulated on the historical eve of a globalized nationalism, it also points forward to the distinction between the entitled *demos* and populations treated as living stock. The uncertainty in the circuit of capital during the pandemic has compelled its explicit iteration, from the talk of "herd immunity" in the UK and elsewhere to the White House adviser Kevin Hassett's statement that "Our human capital stock is ready to go back to work."

What Marx did not envisage was the extent to which capitalism's voracious appetite for surplus-value would subsequently be rationalized through the retrieval of genealogy in understandings of population management, welfare and productivity. From Fordism to neoliberalism, the transformation of the household from economic analogy to financial and heritable asset would diffuse the scope of investments in genealogical accounts of right and cut across the liquidity of the wages and social incomes that had previously defined the condition of the working class. In line with the organicist, political corporation described by Marx in his critique of Hegelian political philosophy, a corresponding nationalism and idea of imperial entitlement would incorporate parts of the working class into the terms of popular sovereignty, or the political-economic and social contract, while excluding others. Moreover if, as Marx suggested, agriculture had furnished the tropes of aristocratic right through primogeniture in late feudalism, in the shift to capitalism it would provide the initial techniques, knowledge and metaphors of population management. Some of the latter would be rehearsed in the more recent history and philosophy of virology, including that of coronaviruses.

The first complete genome sequencing of a sampled prototypical human coronavirus OC43 strain was reported in 2005—after the SARS outbreak in 2002. Along with HCoV-229E, HCoV-OC43 is otherwise known as the common cold. Most of what had been known prior to this about coronaviruses, including the so-called common cold, came from the veterinary and agricultural sciences. The initial report's authors went on to hypothesize that the event of zoonotic transfer between cattle (of the bovine coronavirus) and humans may have occurred as the result of sustained and unprotected human involvement in large culls of cattle in the late nineteenth century. They place the event of transfer sometime around 1873, give or take a decade or more. The culls were undertaken in an effort to stop the collapse of the beef industry due to the spread of a highly infectious cattle disease, and as a means of halting its spread to other herds and cattle around the world.[23] Either way, there were a number of disease outbreaks in agriculture in the late nineteenth century and the use of herd slaughter as a principal technique of disease management. One of the most devastating and widespread being the so-called *rinderpest* (or 'cattle plague'), caused by a virus similar to measles.

This is the history of agribusiness, of land enclosures, and the enormous growth of human populations reliant on wages for their existence (or liquid money rather than heritable assets or capital). That history overlaps with the histories of philosophy, insurance and the welfare state. Often, those overlaps have often been obscured in philosophical accounts of molecular biology.

For instance, in his discussion of transhumanism in *Viroid Life*, Keith Ansell-Pearson attempted to salvage nineteenth-century dirtbag philosopher Friedrich Nietzsche from his justified association with the history of fascism.[24] While he is critical of Nietzsche in some respects, he nevertheless obscures a great deal by removing Nietzsche's writings from their immediate context. In 1886, Nietzsche published *Beyond Good and Evil*, in which he complained that efforts to protect the weak and avert suffering was a "herd" mentality that would prevent the coming of the Übermensch—literally, 'over-man,' a frequent term in German National Socialist self-descriptions as the so-called master race and, as we shall see, a continuing inspiration for the far right.

Briefly, Nietzschean genealogy is an aesthetic philosophy of race plus time, in that it treats race not as a fixed property or being, but a becoming in time, liable therefore to degeneracy or improvement. In that respect, racial genealogy is an analogue of property inheritance and eschatology—a property that can be "mixed" and decay, or achieve the providential realization of its idealized, "noble" origins through the endurance of a purgatorial suffering. Much of the detail of Nietzsche's argument was shaped by debates around the Prussian welfare state and the idea of social insurance—beginning in policy with the Health Insurance bill, passed in 1883, and garnering support among conservative politicians as political insurance against insurrection. These are the origins of the welfare state, the first of its kind in the world. It is the moment in which the problem of the health and welfare of well-defined populations becomes a matter of distinct policy, shaped by citizenship based on land ownership, marriage laws and, in time, immigration policy. The techniques of the latter—in particular, the patrolled line punctuated by detainment at checkpoints—were borrowed from those of the quarantine and the *cordon sanitaire*.

VAG
ABO
NDS

Quarantine

Conceptually, quarantine involves two key features: first, the segregation of populations on the basis of a hypothesis about their exposure and, second, their detainment, usually for a specified period of time, so as to insert a division between exposed and susceptible populations. Unlike case isolation, which separates out particular cases, the quarantine is not based on evidenced infections but enacts a geographic or spatial congregation based on presumed conditions. That is, because 'exposure' is effectively an inference, rather than knowledge based on either testing or the clinical identification of symptoms, its use of proxies as a means of identifying exposure—such as geography or passports—is amenable to the identification of a disease with a group of persons, and therefore the racialization of disease. At the same time, the recourse to travel bans brought into sharp relief the distinction between, on the one hand, epidemiological and clinical methods or laboratory testing for ascertaining knowledge about the existence of the virus—not least of which is the phrase 'community transmission,' and, on the other, the role that national borders play in constituting a terminological (but not quantitative) difference between an epidemic and a pandemic.

However, because the transmission of respiratory infections is exacerbated by people congregating in close-quarters contact for a period of time, the quarantine easily turns into an incubator. An increase in the rate of infection is, for instance, the highly predictable outcome of quarantining cruise ships. So too, in many ways, was an increase in the rate of infection in assisted living facilities, prisons, immigration detention, or at airports which became overcrowded as a result of the announcement of travel bans. In this way, the implication of disease or threat as an imputed intrinsic property of certain groups of people is mysteriously proven in their having been placed in circumstances where they are at higher risk of infection. While initially much was not known about SARS-CoV-2, the inadequacies and dangers of quarantines were foreseeable. The ineffectiveness of quarantine measures in stemming the transmission of diseases and, in some predictable instances facilitating their spread by congregating large numbers of people, could have been mitigated by an early prioritization of widespread testing—that is, by resorting to evidence and treating cases of infection rather than relying on, and promoting, the intuitive epistemology and categorical logic of the quarantine.

Most governments responded to initial reports of a highly-transmissible disease with a high mortality rate by instituting travel restrictions—in effect, an attempt to establish *cordon sanitaire* around city and state borders. The first of these was established by the Chinese government around Wuhan. Other governments announced restrictions on the travel of non-citizens from China—followed by subsequent bans on, say, Iran as the number of reported cases there rose. These measures were adopted far earlier than any other physical interventions in disease transmission—such as the use of masks, or public health advice about the importance of physical distancing and regular handwashing. In most cases, the latter set of relatively inexpensive measures was only adopted due to pressure from epidemiologists, health workers and others. Their effectiveness was however never a secret since the physics of respiratory infection are fairly well-understood. Indeed, according to a model by two epidemiologists, an "estimated 90 percent of the cumulative deaths" in the US, "at least from the first wave of the epidemic, might have been prevented by putting social distancing policies [school closures and limits on the number of people who could congregate] into effect two weeks earlier" than they had been.[25]

Moreover, measures other than quarantine had already been found to be much more effective in preventing the spread of respiratory infections. In a lengthy review of a number of studies on the comparative effectiveness of various measures (short of vaccines and antiviral drugs) to prevent the transmission of respiratory viruses—screening at entry ports, medical isolation, quarantine, social distancing, barriers, personal protection, and hand hygiene—the use of surgical masks and regular handwashing emerged as the most consistently effective set of physical interventions. The review also found that the medical isolation of symptomatic patients was important but that "global measures, such as screening at entry ports, led to a non-significant marginal delay."[26] Further, as one scholar from the Johns Hopkins Center for Health Security warned: "no one should think that there won't be more cases" simply because there is a travel ban. The World Health Organization similarly advised against closing borders as a means of handling the disease. It pointed out that "closing borders was probably ineffective in halting the transmission of the deadly novel coronavirus from China and could even accelerate its spread," in part because punitive approaches make it that much more difficult for health workers to treat cases and track the spread of diseases.[27]

Even if one were to grant the dubious assumption that the transmission of diseases might be halted (or meaningfully slowed) through territorial restrictions on people's mobility, the genomic *identification* of a new strain of virus—while accelerated by the introduction of automated genome sequencing in the 1980s—would invariably occur *after its appearance*. Either way, expenditure and focus on quarantine restrictions represented a prioritization and resourcing of measures least likely to be effective in both the immediate and longer term relative to other measures. That is, quarantines exacerbate viral dangers because they foster the illusion that the isolation of a virus is synonymous with (or achievable through) the spatial confinement of groups of people, whose confinement is determined not by whether they are symptomatic or diagnosed with a disease but by a purportedly preemptive measure that uses geography (and, by implication, nationality and race) as a proxy for exposure. In addition to its known and relative ineffectiveness, accounts of the contemporary recourse to quarantine measures therefore have to explain the widespread willingness by (neoliberal to far right) governments to resort to an intuitive idea of exposure over testing and, given its preemptive and selective constraints on freedom of movement, to emphasize borders as a technique of health.

Neoliberalism

In his 1977 lectures at the Collège de France, Foucault suggested that with the emergence of the concept of population "it will no longer be the problem of exclusion, as with leprosy, or of quarantine, as with the plague, but," he continued, "of epidemics and the medical campaigns that try to halt epidemic or endemic phenomena."[28] To be sure, on a number of occasions he warns of the misguided inclination to treat neoliberalism as a *laissez-faire* doctrine.[29] Nevertheless, he insisted on a shift from territorial sovereignty (marked by the quarantine) to a deterritorialized security. Therefore, despite various efforts to complicate the historical schema he presents, the crux of the problem is his treatment of modern "biopolitics" as the politicization of life, understood as the imposition of a political rationality on life as such—and not, by contrast, a metaphysical idea of life whose assumption is that of the *oikos*. It is an approach that becomes amplified in his later lectures and writings in which he romanticized the noble household.

It is also a view derived from Christian theology, and which has animated economic liberalism from its earliest expressions in the work of Francis Hutcheson and Smith to the neoliberalism of Friedrich Hayek and Gary Becker. In all, political rule is associated with an intolerable, unnatural imposition on the autonomy of self-regulating patriarchal households. Particularly in his later writings, Foucault is broadly uncritical toward the idea of the household as the diffusion rather than the eclipse of sovereignty—that is, the preservation of a genealogical inscription through which 'every man becomes a king in his own castle.' That this diffuse sovereignty is intensified under conditions—not of an epidemic or in medical campaigns to fight endemic diseases—but of a pandemic is the culmination of the tendency of neoliberalism to privatize health and displace the risks of disease through a generalized system of households understood as the elementary units of national economies and the analogy of international trade relations. It renders legitimate genealogies inscribed in private property laws and patterns of inherited wealth into the premise of neoliberal health policy.[30] It also blends the privatization of risk with those colonial and slave-holding systems of authoritarian governance that regard populations as in need of paternalistic 'protection.' These same systems are incapable of the deliberative foresight that, in the structuring of legal personhood, has been considered the necessary attribute of responsible property-ownership and entitlement.

The quarantine did not exactly disappear throughout the twentieth century.[31] Rather, it persisted at the anxious, colonial margins of a classical European taxonomic machinery and legal personhood. In colonial contexts the quarantine remained a technology and metaphor preoccupied with defining and managing a perceived vulnerable purity placed under the prudent protection of colonial administrators.[32]

Examples from the settler colony of Australia are instructive. On the one hand, the quarantine technique of detainment for a specified period of time was relegated to the handling of flora and fauna at entry ports, particularly where it concerned the protection of agricultural products and markets, or threats from microbial and other species of plant and animal designated as exotic or invasive. It is a distorted articulation of preservation by one of the most concentrated systems of agribusiness in the world—remarkable, given the enormously destructive impact of English farming and crops such as wheat on the extinction of species of plants and animals that existed prior to colonization.

On the other hand, in 2007–08 the quarantine reappeared as a trope of racial welfare policy—as with the "quarantining" of welfare payments to Indigenous people in Australia. Replacing access to liquid or cash payments with a so-called basics card (a plastic card that could only make purchases at designated places such as supermarkets), it eliminated the capacity of Indigenous people in northern Australia to decide what to purchase and where throughout the Northern Territory and in four Cape York communities. Prior to this, Indigenous people in Australia had been excluded from social security schemes well into the twentieth century or, in many cases, had their welfare and wages placed into government accounts whose disbursement was tightly controlled.[33] The changes to welfare in 2007–08 represented a return to compulsory income management. The legislation fostered "the view that Indigenous people's lack of financial capacity was creating poverty" and "socially responsible behavior, particularly in relation to the care and education of children," and that this should be remedied by "paternalistic prohibitions on spending."[34] The points of convergence between the agricultural quarantine and the "quarantining" of welfare is the inclination of colonial policy toward separation and 'protection'. Until 1967 in Australia, Indigenous people were not counted in the census but, more or less explicitly, "grouped along with native flora and fauna" and, prior to this, "counted along with stock" in the inventories of agricultural properties.[35] Indeed, the paternalistic notion of protection obscures the introduction of novel diseases for which there was no immunity among Indigenous people by early colonists and the prolonged effort to convert a continent and populations into the docile, productive objects of British imperial supply-chains—in particular the production of wool and cotton destined for British mills.

As a formalized practice, quarantines first appeared in mid-fourteenth-century Europe during the so-called Black Death or bubonic plague. The pandemic was so-named because of the appearance of blackened pustules at the site of flea bites and swollen lymph nodes. A bacterial infection (*yersinia pestis*), it could be spread through septicemic and pneumonic transmission. As it moved across Europe, the Middle East, and parts of Asia, it is estimated to have resulted in the deaths of around 50 million people. The Black Death figures prominently in the emergence of capitalism from feudalism, representing the idea of an enormous epochal shift—and therefore a source of trepidation and analogy in understandings of the current pandemic.

At the time, the prevalent theory of transmissible diseases held that they were caused by miasma—a poisonous vapor in which there were suspended particles of decaying matter that caused a foul smell. While the miasma theory prompted some beneficial sanitation measures, it also dangerously conflated cleanliness (to the naked eye and the nose) with the absence of transmissible, contagious diseases and, conversely, promoted the mistaken view that the presence of contagious diseases could be identified by observing a lack of cleanliness.

As for the quarantine, its name is derived from the Latin for 'forty', *quadraginta*. It stipulated 40 days segregation, and was derived from Christian theologies of sin and redemption, in which plagues were understood as divine punishment on a fallen world, and separation from the world was seen as a physical act of submission to providential care, devotion and God's judgment. There are frequent references to 40 days in the Bible, the most notable being the story of Noah's Ark and the flooding rains, and Jesus's period of suffering in the wilderness.

The increasing recourse to quarantine measures did not stem or bring an end to the Black Death. Nor did they halt the subsequent outbreaks of infectious diseases that would recur in enormous lethal waves for some three centuries, would reappear well into the eighteenth, and occur again with the so-called Spanish influenza at the beginning of the twentieth century. While the origins of the 'Spanish' influenza continue to be a matter of debate, what is known is that, for instance, quarantined ships would stop people aboard from disembarking, and so become the terrible plague ships that appeared to affirm the quarantine measure through public spectacles of extreme human suffering purportedly kept at a distance. Yet they did not stop bacteria-infected fleas from hopping off ships aboard smaller animals such as rats, or the spread of the pestis by other means. Significant declines in mortality from this time have largely been due to the development of effective public health measures (such as changes in funerary and burial practices, the handling of dead animals, and refuse collection), a more accurate understanding of the mechanisms of disease transmission and, in time, the powerful but arguably overly-prescribed use of antibiotics.

Historians will continue to debate the social,
cultural and economic impact of the Black
Death—the decline of the Holy Roman Empire
and Protestant Reformation, the Renaissance,
the rise of epidemiology and public health, and
the transformation of agriculture in the course of
what some have described as "a 300-year period
of ecological crisis" that shook the late medieval
period.[36] These three centuries are the regular
staging grounds for rival hypotheses about the
emergence of capitalism, industrialization and
wage labor, as well as theories about depopulation and ecological-economic limits. They are
also, however, a reminder that explanations of
the SARS-CoV-2 pandemic which frame it as the
result of modernity are, to put it mildly, nonsen-
sical. For while the contemporary pandemic has
prompted Malthusian-inspired ecofascists to cele-
brate depopulation, this history is a reminder that
Malthus elaborated both a moral economy, as we
shall see, derived from medieval biblical eschatology (a theory of the end-times) and, in the detail,
an anti-modernist nostalgia for the times when
diseases would keep the poor in check.

The systematic use of the quarantine—as a
spatial technique imbued with disciplinary and
providential powers—became a key inspiration
for efforts to stem the breakdown of the Medieval
order, despite its ineffectiveness in relation to
disease transmission. On the one hand, the waves
of pandemics eroded a tangible faith in the
eternal existence of a universe of ranked superi-
ority. It was the universe imaginatively depicted
as natural by the taxonomic hierarchy of the *scala*

natura. In reality, that was a diagram which idealized the mundane, feudal systems of bonded and heritable servitude that had furnished a relatively stable and cross-generational workforce for large agricultural estates. On the other hand, it is throughout this period that laws restricting the movements of people—and agricultural workers in particular—were slowly assembled across the moving patchwork of European states and church parishes. Those laws included such things as the introduction of passes (a nascent system of passports), the criminalization of vagabondage (of those who had *vaga-* or 'wandered' from their presumably natural bond with their masters), and the forging of bureaucratic and conditional links between access to charity and the recording of place of birth in parish registries.

Cordon Sanitaire

The medieval emphasis on detainment in the quarantine eventually merged with eighteenth-century public hygiene campaigns—and the sanitary logic of the nineteenth-century *cordon sanitaire*, or 'line of hygiene' that involves a clearly-defined and policed or militarized limit on the geographic movement of groups of people. The term '*cordon sanitaire*' was first used in 1821, when the French Restoration monarchy deployed some 30,000 troops at the Franco-Spanish border on the pretext of preventing the spread of yellow fever into France. It figured prominently in conservative efforts to split nationalists from their support for republicanism (and its hostility to monarchical rule) through heightened geopolitical conflict at the border. More broadly, the *cordon sanitaire* represents a tightening between the territorial logic of sovereignty, the spatial logic of the quarantine, and eighteenth-century hygienics.

This history, however, involves both forks and mergers. It is possible to draw a line from these policies to the development of biosecurity, from those that emphasize threats to agricultural industries and exports, to the more recent focus on bioterrorism and military preparedness. But for much of the twentieth century the techniques of applying, on the one hand, a physical barrier against disease transmission between individuals and, on the other, the militarized line of hygiene would diverge. The recent history of the condom, small-scale and mobile testing technologies, PPE and the hazmat suit all point to that divergence and a widespread view concerning the unreliability of policing and militarized border practices in stemming infectious diseases.

A crucial turning-point in this history was the *cordon sanitaire* in West Africa with the appearance of Ebola from 2013–16. It sharpened a conflict between global and national health governance, foregrounded the role and interests in global health governance, and—as in the lockdown in Freetown, Sierra Leone in 2015—echoed the repressive smallpox campaigns of earlier times and resulted in harsh, military responses to protests over food shortages in the quarantined zone. In late 2014, at an emergency meeting between the governments of Liberia, Guinea and Sierra Leone, it was decided that a triangular area in which there were the vast majority (some 70 percent) of confirmed cases and which crossed the borders of each state, a triangular area would be designated as a quarantine zone and locked down. The World Health Organization cautioned against human rights abuses but did not publicly oppose the plan. The plan, in effect, was to allow the disease to run its course (and presumably 'burn out') within a zone whose boundary was enforced by troops, while offering minimal care and treatment to around 30 percent of cases outside the triangle.

The reappearance of the quarantine in West Africa was no doubt accompanied by a range of meanings, yet one stands out. The decision to partition a geographic area was made on the basis of the most densely-shaded part of the cluster of confirmed cases of infection visible on a map, and included many people who had not been infected, with obviously tragic consequences. That was premised on decisions about the limited availability of healthcare and testing—whose capacity to grow beyond existing limits was restricted by a sharp line drawn on a map and troops on the ground with which that line was enforced. As one doctor put it: "It seems like a reflexive movement by the governments to show that they're doing something, and since they have armies more elaborate than their health care systems, they use the army."[37]

While the quarantine may have been pushed to the margins of legal personhood and health governance throughout the twentieth century, its reappearance represents the merger of methods of authoritarian population governance with the idea of private, selective healthcare. Indeed, Trump's appointment of Robert Redfield as director of the Centers for Disease Control and Prevention illustrates the meaning of this *selection*: that is, the 'spontaneous' resort to quarantine—as a spatial technique imbued with both disciplinary and providential powers—and opposition to unqualified, evidenced healthcare as if this represents the facilitation of moral risk and disorder.[38] During his tenure as an army doctor at Walter Reed Medical Center, Redfield argued that soldiers with HIV/AIDS should be quarantined—in accord with the Christian Right group with which he was associated, Americans for a Sound HIV/AIDS Policy (ASAP). A conservative Catholic, Redfield had also contended that "the breakdown of the American family" was a key factor in the spread of AIDS because it encouraged promiscuity. Moreover, according to ASAP it was necessary "to reject false prophets who preach the quick-fix strategies of condoms and free needles" and "those who try to replace God as judge."[39]

VĀG
ABO
NDS

Bodies in Motion

Some five months prior to the appearance of
SARS-CoV-2, the far-right magazine *Quillette* published a lengthy, effusive profile on Brexit champion
and then-presumptive British prime minister Boris
Johnson, who had recently won his Conservative
party's backing as leader. Its associate editor, Toby
Young, wrote that "with his imposing physical
build, his thick neck and his broad, Germanic
forehead, there was also something of Nietzsche's
Übermensch about" Johnson, adding, "an almost
tangible will to power." *Quillette,* which recycles
reactionary ideas while claiming to be a besieged
bastion of neutral rationality and freedom of
expression, had already achieved quite a repu-
tation for repackaging and promoting eugenics,
anthropometry, and similar approaches which
used physical or statistical measures to explain
away inequalities as inborn characteristics and the
expression of racial or other presumably immuta-
ble differences.[40] Young was keen to wonder
whether Johnson "is the right man to lead Britain
at this moment of maximum danger," by which
he meant the final decision on Brexit.[41] How the
political right understands and defines "maximum
danger" is certainly a worthwhile question. Yet, it
is one that, in both Brexit and the approach toward
SARS-CoV-2 adopted by the UK government,

hinged on a convergence between neoliberal, national-populist and far-right descriptions of 'the people' and perceived threats to their health.

Contrary to the posture of imperious and fearless decisiveness, deliberate inaction, incompetence or a negligent complacency reigned in the first and crucial months. The *Sunday Times* published a damning, detailed account of how Johnson decided not to attend briefings on the virus throughout February, ignored calls to order protective gear, and failed to heed scientists' warnings about the seriousness of the disease.[42] The editor of *The Lancet*, Richard Hornton, accused the UK government of "deliberately rewriting history in its ongoing Covid-19 disinformation campaign," including its failure to resolve impending shortages of intensive care units it had been warned of in late January.[43]

By early April, Johnson was hospitalized after testing positive for the virus. Officially, this was a "precautionary move." Perhaps Johnson was in a serious condition, perhaps not. Who knows. The precautionary principle, however, is at odds with Johnson's trademark providential optimism. It was this performative optimism, said to conjure its own material conditions into being, that had informed the government's stated intention, in March, to allow the virus to spread among those designated, on the basis of statistical averages of groups as 'at least risk' of dying in order to promote "herd immunity." It was not, however, entirely at odds with the personalized exemption offered by a blunt reading of the seventeenth-century philosopher Thomas Hobbes's theory of

popular sovereignty and the political contract—
and according to which one journalist invited
readers to identify their own and the nation's
health with the "naked vulnerability" of the prime
minister's body.[44] Meanwhile, the UK government
was denying reports that the policy it had
articulated in private meetings was, in summary,
"herd immunity, protect the economy, and if that
means some pensioners die, too bad."[45]

Thanks in part to decades of neoliberal
cutbacks for which Johnson's Conservatives bear
no small measure of responsibility, there was no
capacity for widespread testing in the UK. Nor
would everyone have access to the level and precautionary hospitalization available to Johnson
had they been found to have tested positive. This
was doubly true thanks to the "hostile environment" policy against undocumented migrants
into which the healthcare system had been con-
scripted, and the prohibitive additional fees for
healthcare for migrants in general, who already
pay taxes to support that system. Moreover, given
the repeated chances of contact with infection,
equipment shortages, limited testing and the
preponderance of non-white and migrant staff
in the UK's health system, the dangers for those
who worked in healthcare were both particularly
stark and heavily weighted along racial lines. By
mid-April, ten doctors in the UK had died from
Covid-19. Not one of them was white.[46]

Herd Immunity

Around ten weeks after the initial identification
of the novel coronavirus, on March 13, the UK's

chief science advisor, Patrick Vallance, explained that it would be necessary to "build up some kind of herd immunity so more people are immune to this disease and we reduce the transmission."[47] It was not an admission that 'containment' had failed in both its assumption that 'community transmission' was insignificant and in its logic or techniques. Rather, it would be the "next stage" and, at a higher level of abstraction, a continuation of its unreliable logic.

By that logic, since the virus had slipped the lines of racial-national genealogy with increasing rates of 'community transmission,' it might somehow be persuaded to providentially distribute its varied risks (of ill-health, mortality, and immunity) according to statistical classes. That statistical averages only function through large numbers—and therefore lose their predictive strength at the level of individuals who actually become ill or infected—did not appear to concern those for whom the categories of 'at risk' or 'at least risk' would be presented as a guide for the assumption of 'personal responsibility.' As with the concept of 'containment', "herd immunity's" use in this instance tended to assume a well-described population composed of well-defined, relatively non-mixing classes with predictably averaged responses to infection—that is, the risk profile of statistical classes. When linked to vaccination programs, "herd immunity" can be a theoretically useful but imprecise concept.[48] In the absence of a vaccine, it is profoundly terrible.

While "herd immunity" did not appear in any report on which the government claimed to base its approach, it was nevertheless implicit in the strategy outlined by Johnson, and explicitly put forward by Vallance as an implausible explanation of why the government would not move to a partial shutdown of schools, venues and some workplaces. According to Vallance, the strategy would "allow enough of us who are going to get mild illness to become immune and [for] this to help with the whole population response which would protect everybody." The number he proposed, "the sort of figure you need to get herd immunity," would "probably be around sixty percent or so" of the population—around 36 million people. The Dutch prime minister echoed this approach on March 17, suggesting that the Netherlands was looking at the "controlled distribution" of the virus "among groups that are least at risk" of dying from infection.

Given the number of hypotheticals involved—including whether the risk profiles were accurate given the data was mostly anecdotal at this point—it is impossible to accord this with much credence. Nevertheless, the functioning of congregating spaces like workplaces, entertainment venues, schools, prisons and detention facilities were to be maintained, and this would be presented as a plausible public health policy. Claims that a "controlled distribution" could accomplish "herd immunity" were made in the absence of knowledge as to whether immunity through prior infection with an unmodified virus was indeed possible, and what the implications of such an approach would be—including for the health of each infected person and those with whom they

had contact, and for the capacity of the healthcare system.

The crux of the problem was that, firstly, "herd immunity" involves the certified administration of a modified virus in order to prompt the creation of antibodies in a sufficiently large number of individuals in a population that an outbreak is mitigated. Secondly, in the absence of a vaccine, the UK government intended to rely instead on a combination of (the capacity for) privatized or self-managed risk assessment and the facilitation of infection across non-randomly mixing and designated risk categories of the population. All this while rationing the use of non-pharmaceutical interventions, including failing to increase intensive care beds. Presumably well-defined categories of risk and their averages would furnish the (theoretical) knowledge according to which everyone would be advised to (and indeed could) take their presumably well-informed chances and, not least, personally bear the risks of those decisions.

It was, bluntly, a distinctly neoliberal approach in at least three ways: First, it emphasized the apparent statistical average that working-age adults were at lower risk of serious illness or of dying from infection. Second, it advanced a theory that schools might serve as open-air laboratories (and children's bodies, the medium) through which to modify or weaken the virus in some hypothetical moment prior to its transmission. Finally, it placed the onus on self-regulating households and individual calculations of largely unknown risks.

But it is also illustrative of the pivots between neoliberal and far-right understandings of chance. As we now know, the effects of this policy were that, by April 19, the UK had an overall and confirmed case fatality rate of 13.32 percent—that is, the number of deaths as a proportion of a hundred confirmed cases of infection. It was, at the time, the second-worst confirmed case fatality rate in the world.[49] It may have been worse had the UK government not been forced to alter its course, at least publicly and half-heartedly. Confronted at the time with growing and increasingly scathing criticism, and the release of modeling by the Imperial College Covid-19 Response Team (which strongly argued for an alternative approach of rapid and indefinite suppression instead), the UK government changed tack on March 25 and ordered a partial shutdown.

The Imperial College report's main finding was that even the most extreme mitigation approach—involving case isolation, household quarantine and social distancing of the elderly—would likely mean that the surge limits for both general ward and intensive care beds would be exceeded by a factor of eight over/under the best scenario for critical care requirements. Even if all patients could be treated under this scenario, they predicted that there would still be around a quarter of a million deaths in the UK—and over a million deaths in the US. The goal of suppression, in contrast to that of mitigation, would be to indefinitely interrupt transmission (that is, to bring the daily multiplication of cases to below zero). That would mean the addition of widespread testing and tracking, a shift to online work where possible, a surge in the supply and use of non-pharmaceutical interventions and any available medical treatments and, contrary to the approach favored by the Johnson government, a partial and indefinite economic shutdown until the development of a vaccine.

The difference between the government's distorted "herd immunity" approach and the suppression strategy advanced by Imperial College was, ironically, that the latter assumed a conventional definition of "herd immunity." By that conventional definition, "herd immunity" is the numerical answer to a mathematical formulation about the necessary threshold of *vaccine-rendered* immunity in a given population, the precise number of which would be sufficient to render the average number of secondary transmissions too few for an infection to spread. It is a mathematical model used to guide vaccination programs. Unlike the distorted "herd immunity" theory advanced by the UK government, because it presupposes the existence of a vaccine it assumes a high degree of knowledge about how immunity comes about. The government's concept of "herd immunity" was, by contrast, far closer to that of anti-vaccination campaigners who promote the use of parties as a means of their children privately (and providentially) acquiring an immunity to diseases such as measles—while pointedly not participating in interrupting the chances of transmission of those diseases to others in the meantime. In addition to an enormous number of unknowns on which this purportedly natural facilitation of infection and immunity were premised, there is, moreover, neither a vaccine (which serves as the actual "herd immunity" buffer in the case of measles), nor is there a standard course of antiviral or other pharmacological treatments and available healthcare capacity that might serve to catch those who do not become immune.

Indeed, the misnamed "herd immunity" strategy would, despite the government's claims of protecting the vulnerable, actively enable the virus to cut a predictable path of destruction through existing patterns of private household wealth, ill-health and mortality exacerbated by decades of neoliberal policy—and call it a natural disaster. The UK government had, in other words, managed to redescribe a concept derived from twentieth-century epidemiology as if it were a eugenic program *purportedly* ruled by chance. Given the known patterns of ill-health and disease, it was one whose outcomes would hew close to disparities in private household wealth and access to healthcare; and one that, in turn, would vastly increase the chances of transmission to those who worked in those sectors that maintained and linked the purportedly private life of households. Thus the fallacy of Malthus' concept of 'surplus populations' is made real through the active creation of distinct life-chances.

The government's approach has been grounded in a theory of population with a long history—one whose trace can be found in both exoticist explanations of SARS-CoV-2 (as discussed above) and an epidemiological language whose terminology is framed not just by national healthcare systems, but

nationalism—as with 'community transmission,'
or the endogeneity implicit to the terms 'endemic'
and 'epidemics,' in contrast to the anthropological and populist divisions assumed by 'pandemic,'
from the Greek for 'all' (*pan*) and 'peoples' (*demos*).
As it happens, the history of population theory is
also the history of political contract theory and
the idea of popular sovereignty.

Hobbes

Hobbes did not take the divine or natural right of
kings as his point of departure. It was not simply
the English Civil War which made that seem
untenable. As important as this was, Hobbes's
fascination with the science of bodies in motion
and anatomy explains far more of the character
of his response to that conflict—one in which
the combination of successive anti-feudal uprisings and plagues conspired to shatter theologies
of an eternal, hierarchically-ranked universe that
had, until that point, been represented by the biological hierarchy of the *scala naturae*.[50] Hobbes's
distinctive question was how to preserve property
rights, including the entitlements of a monarchical empire. For this, Hobbes invents the idea of
a political contract and popular sovereignty. By
these terms, the legitimacy of governments is
open to question and conflict—but not that of
a defined people and the presumably mysterious
ways in which they come about as such; nor the
sovereign whose body is said to personify the unity
of that people.

Drawing on the astronomy of Galileo, Copernicus and Gassendi, as well as early anatomical sciences, Hobbes's logical procedure is concerned with the gravitational forces and motion of bodies, their physiological motivations, and the circulatory, nutritive movements within the 'organic' body politic of the commonwealth.[51] In *Leviathan*, while he often turns to organic analogies for the political, he nevertheless sought to establish a scientific basis for political legitimacy in what ultimately becomes a conventionalist account of sovereign rule—the "Artificial Man the Common-wealth"—through a "geometric" procedure of abstraction. Unlike antiquarian natural philosophies, the course of Hobbes's reasoning ascends from the microscopic to the macroscopic. That is, he proceeded from atomistic premises regarding the physiological nature of man (the "laws of motion of bodies"), toward an argument for the composition of the Many (a multitude of self-sovereign individuals) into the sovereign, popular One. In summary, Hobbes's political philosophy is premised on a concept of bodies in motion (the dissolution of the eternal arrangement of those bodies), the preservation of property and deliberative foresight.[52]

Hobbes's theory is important to parse because it contains three of the key tenets of later population theory that remain influential in both statistics and political contract theory: atomism, categorical aggregation and prediction. From the premise of atomism, Hobbes goes on to argue for the necessity of authoritarian sovereign command over the movements of bodies and desires in the name of the order, prosperity and vitality of the governed population—an authority transferred to the sovereign through the implied contractual assent of the governed, in which the aggregate unity of the society is personified by the sovereign's body. The Hobbesian political contract is the means by which the preservation of private property—and the merchants who serve as Hobbes's analogy for the delegated transacting authority of the masters of households—becomes the keystone of political rule and legitimacy.

Malthus

Derived from Hobbes's "geometric" account of bodies in motion, physiology, and a theology of natural law, Malthusian population theory in the eighteenth century brought the plenum down from the heavens, imbued animate, worldly bodies with a teleology deduced from the gravitational-physiological forces of appetites and aversions, and fostered a distinctive eschatology which ran as follows: in the absence of a regulative aversion to death—implicitly, meaning absent a fear of divine punishment and an eternal, posthumous hell and, therefore, conducive to a deficiency in the self-governing, prudential faculty of deliberative foresight—catastrophe is the inevitable outcome. Aggregated, a deficiency of 'personal responsibility' within the self-government of 'bodies in motion' no longer marks a private crisis of (patriarchal, productive) households but heralds an impending social catastrophe of biblical proportions.

This is the point at which, in the paradigm of economic liberalism, Smith's providential invisible hand gives way to Malthus's eschatological, political-economic and punitive fist. In the historical sweep of economic liberalism, that turning-point is the revolution and uprisings in France and the French colonies. Malthus was the most vociferous and influential exponent for turning purportedly unproductive, unchecked bodies in motion toward properly productive ends—unchecked, that is, by the prudential restraint of sex before marriage, through "want of necessaries which mainly stimulates the labouring class," through the forced labor of the workhouse, or the recurrence of catastrophes such as "plagues, famines, and mortal epidemics."[53]

At the center of Malthus's argument was the now-familiar exponential graph. Discussing the "prodigious power of increase in plants and animals," Malthus contended that "their natural tendency must be to increase in a geometrical ratio, that is, by multiplication; and at whatever rate they are increasing during any period, if no further obstacles be opposed to them, they must proceed in a geometrical progression."[54] It encodes teleology in a rudimentary mathematical formula, where everything is understood to obey a natural law of multiplication, unless, that is, its "geometric" multiplication is checked by the (clerical) foresight granted by a knowledge of that (implicitly divine) law. This is the gist of the Malthusian 'natural limit.'

For Malthus, that purportedly natural limit was the price of bread. When Boris Johnson was still a backbencher in 2007, he penned an article in the *Telegraph* in which he claimed that "global over-population" was the most important issue, and the real cause of food unaffordability.[55]

Epidemiological Mathematics

Most conventional understandings of "herd immunity" draw on the work of John Fox and others in the early 1970s, for whom it meant "the resistance of a group to attack by a disease to which a large proportion of the members are immune, thus lessening the likelihood of a patient with a disease coming into contact with a suscep- tible individual."[56] As Paul Fine points out, that definition is open to interpretations that become less clear depending on the infectious agent, mech- anisms of transmission and the manner in which immunity is possible in each instance. Either way, "herd immunity" by that definition became the number in a mathematical formulation or series of questions that could be modeled and guide public health vaccination programs. According to Fox, in "the planning of such programs, if they are to be of maximum effectiveness," what would have to be the known (calculable and estimated) factors in its operation.[57] According to Fine, the first use of the term "herd immunity" is in a 1923 paper by William Topley and Graham Wilson. For Topley and Wilson, it remained a question; and one that could not be answered in the absence of "inoculation" by "a protective serum."[58]

While it is not the focus of Fine's discussion of the history of epidemiological mathematics, it is important to bear in mind that there can be no floating enumerator in well-formed statistical statements. Conversely put, there has to be some way of defining *a* population, limit or constant against which variables are expressed and measured. As the French statistician Alain Desrosières has shown, statistical statements, including those of epidemiological mathematics, assume a bounded, abstract space of comparability and equivalence—though he draws few links to the connections between statistical knowledge and the history and borders of population control.[59] Nevertheless, systems of governance draw mundane connections between the abstract space of equivalence operationalized by statistical knowledge and money as a general equivalent—and it is one in which the limits of equivalence (or equality) required by asymmetric contracts (the processes of extracting surplus value and shifting risk) have long been situated at the boundaries of the hierarchical *oikos*.[60]

In the history of epidemiological mathematics, on some occasions that bounded space of equivalence has been treated as the assumption of a closed population, as a function of the introduction of immigration restrictions, or as the boundaries of racial classification. On other occasions, that limit is resources. For Malthus, as noted, the 'natural limit' was the price of bread. In arguments to 'flatten the (epidemiological) curve,' that fixed limit is the assumed invariable capacity of a national healthcare system. That is, there are points in these mathematical formulations that abstractly encode a given (and therefore changeable) limit as if it were a constant.

For the theory of "herd immunity" to develop into a general theory of mathematical epidemiology, it would—as Fine argues—require the convergence of three theories and their associated formulations. The first of these is the so-called epidemiological law of mass action. It gives a rudimentary breakdown of an assumed closed population. Borrowed from descriptions of the 'laws of physics,' it is mathematically expressed as a relationship between three numbers in a total population: the total population is equal to those who are susceptible to infection, plus the number of infections, plus the number of those who are immune.

The second step in this development was the case reproduction rate, which is expressed as the epidemiological curve. Developed by George Macdonald in his studies of malaria, it is expressed as the average number of secondary cases who contract an infection from a single case in a totally susceptible population. Macdonald called this the "basic case reproduction rate," and he did so by analogy with the demographic concept of the "intrinsic reproduction rate"—that is, the average number of human progeny if there were no checks on reproduction. The "intrinsic reproduction rate" was central to Malthus's theory of overpopulation.

Subsequent to its infamous use by Malthus, there are two key moments in the demographic formulation of the basic reproduction number. The first is generally attributed to the late-nineteenth-century Prussian statistician Richard Böckh; the second to Dublin and Lotka, who in the 1920s began their discussion by emphasizing the role of new immigration restrictions in delineating the so-called natural rate of population growth from the presumably artificial growth brought about by migration. Dublin and Lotka moreover based their figures on the reproductive potential of white women in the US.[61]

When it is used to predict the spread of infectious diseases, unlike the theory of mass action the basic reproduction number does not presuppose a closed population or, like the theory of mass action, yield a number that is a proportion of a population. What it does do in the now well-known epidemiological curve is reinscribe, in the form of a diagram, something close to a theory of natural limits—usually represented by a straight red line of healthcare capacity that runs horizontally through the curves.

The third step in the history of epidemiological mathematics was the heterogeneous population simulation approach, or Reed-Frost model. Again, unlike the theory of mass action it did not assume a closed population. It did, however, reintroduce a well-defined population by way of reckoning the number for a susceptible population. In this formulation, the constant would be rendered as the "probability of effective contact," or: "the probability that any two individuals in the population have, in one time period (serial interval), the sort of contact necessary for transmission of the infection in question." It was a formulation developed at the Johns Hopkins University School of

Hygiene and Public Health, put forward by Fox et al., and was influential in guiding World Health vaccination programs from the early 1970s.[62]

The innovation of the Reed-Frost model was that it assumed a degree of regular non-mixing within a given population. The statistical name for such distinct groups is classes or categories to which a degree of risk can be assigned. It therefore implies geographies of class, race and households inasmuch as it refers to intimate contact over a given period of time. It measures the chances of contact where those chances are not evenly spread across a total population. Used in the context of a vaccination program, it can mean targeting the administration of a vaccine through fractional sampling.

The UK's "herd immunity" approach was premised on this though, significantly, not as a means of targeting vaccinations but instead as a technique of facilitating purportedly less-risky infections. On March 13, when the UK's chief science advisor was asked why there was no advice against or prohibitions placed on congregating in large groups, he effectively made an argument for the Reed-Frost model and against the theory of mass action. He began by claiming that "the UK has done a good job of contact tracing and isolating," and had advised people to self-isolate at home if they had any symptoms. By early March, it had become unclear whether transmission was possible in a pre-symptomatic stage. Moreover, since he later admitted in the same interview that the total number of cases of infection in the UK was unknown, what he meant by "good job of contact tracing" presumably was of those who had traveled from or had contact with someone who had traveled. The reigning assumption was that there was little "community spread," meaning beyond those who had contact with people in China. All these measures, he insisted, would—"according to the modeling"—have a significant effect on flattening the epidemiological curve but, he went on to add, while "mass gatherings of course are a place where you can potentially get [an] infection ... most of the transmission of these types of viruses occur in small gatherings not in big gatherings."[63]

It stands to reason that close contact over a period of time increases the chances of transmission. But if this is true, it also holds true of many workplaces and restaurants, and certainly holds for crowded spaces such as public transport, prisons, detention centers, care facilities, and, depending on the architecture of housing, households. In other words, while the UK government did not assume a closed population, it nevertheless assumed a relatively non-mixing population—in this instance, the existence of spatial geographies and architectures of race, ethnicity and class.

The government did not make this assumption so as to decide on the best manner in which to distribute a vaccine throughout the UK by way of sampling. Rather, it did so as a way of encouraging infection under the pretext of an experiment for developing a fictive "herd immunity" and therefore by way of presumably "naturally existing conditions"—that is, the very thing that Topley and Wilson had ruled out in 1923 as "impossible."[64] According to figures released on April 21, a disproportionate number of deaths in the UK were of non-white people.[65]

Statistics, Class and Racial Classification

How one interprets figures as that above depends on how one understands statistical classification. For conservatives, and particularly for the far right, statistical methods are not mathematical conventions and incomplete maps so much as more or less adequate representations of independently real or natural categories that, by the logic of intrinsic properties and ranks, are imbued with teleological significance. For racists, mortality rates in which non-white people are over-represented serve as evidence of racial inferiority, just as higher rates of imprisonment have been presented as proof of an intrinsic criminality or, conversely, where dubious claims of an increase in the mortality rates of white people in the US have served as an argument for racial senescence.

It is the point at which statistics merges with anthropometry (including that championed by *Quillette*) and, at the same time, a point of sharp distinction between far-right and Marxist understandings of class and classification. Recalling Marx's embrace of Darwin's non-teleological account of taxonomic categories discussed briefly above: according to Marx and Engels the working class is a class without property and therefore "not recognized as a class" according to a classical logic of essences. It is for this reason that they treated its revolutionary significance not as the normative or inevitable unfolding of an intrinsic property but, instead, as "the expression of the dissolution of all classes, nationalities, etc. within present society." They went on to describe communism as the real movement of the property-less that abolishes "the rule of all classes."[66] Since the late nineteenth century, conservative and far-right understandings of statistical classes have involved reinstating the epistemic assumptions of status and caste—in logical terms: where categories (such as class or nation) are seen as repositories of an intrinsic property, from which it is possible to derive norms and a universal, ranked order, and according to which an originary essence dictates both a necessary law and inevitable fate.

The principal exponent of the far-right view of statistics was Corrado Gini—Mussolini's demographer, titular mathematician of the Gini coefficient (which measures social inequality), and the author of "The Scientific Basis of Fascism" in 1927. For Gini, the measure of social inequality was a measure of the health of the nation, and one explicitly linked in his view to the reproduction of the race. In his 1927 essay, he proposed to shift population statistics from the assumption that "society consists of an aggregate of individuals," in which the state is "the emanation of the individual wills intended to eliminate the conflicts between the interests of individuals," to one in which society is understood as "a true and distinct organism of a rank superior to that of the individuals who compose it, an organism endowed with a life of its own and with interests of its own."[67]

Much of this hinged on measures of Italian female fertility, the national birthrate and fears of racial senescence. According to Gini, the treatment of the nation as an organic entity was the difference between liberal and "nationalistic" understandings of population. More accurately, Gini split Hobbes's atomistic premise from Hobbes's goal of uniting those atomized bodies in an indivisible sovereign rule. This elision made it possible for Gini to argue for the elimination of the social contract as the basis of political legitimacy—and he did so by rendering Hobbes's organic metaphor as a literal biological description. According to Gini, the nation is a living organism, and statistics takes its vital productive and reproductive measures. His argument for "the scientific basis" of fascism, then, is that the legitimacy of the fascist seizure of power (the attempted coup, limitations on the franchise, and government on the basis of a minority of support) is "scientifically" justified because it serves the goal of restoring the organic unity and health of the nation. Where Hobbes emphasized the preservation of private property through the political contract, Gini stressed the preservation of the nation's racial properties through normative sexual reproduction and masculine productivity.

Nietzsche's writings, like Gini's, were steeped in similar questions of racial senescence—or 'white decline.' It is their immediate contexts and influences which differed. Gini's arguments for an increase in the national birthrate were addressed to circumstances of over a million dead and frustrated colonial ambitions in the wake of World War I. Nietzsche's arguments for abandoning 'the weak of the herd' were made in late-nineteenth-century Prussia and a rising German nationalism embroiled in a *kulturkampf* (the original 'culture war') around the boundaries and demography of a projected greater German empire. Moreover, where Catholicism dictated an emphasis on reproduction and the Italian birth-rate, Prussian Protestantism stressed personal responsibility as the method of providential selection.

Some five years before Nietzsche wrote *Beyond Good and Evil*, Richard Böckh, the highly contro-versial head of Prussia's statistical bureau, was promoting a Herderian, linguistic definition of nationality.[68] He argued that everyone who spoke German should be counted as German, including those outside of Prussia. As capacious as Böckh's approach was compared to a growing antisemitism in Europe, the concern with preserving a per-ceived vulnerable purity was nevertheless linked to the imperial project of a greater Germany at a time when a German nation, as such, did not exist in Europe.

In *Beyond Good and Evil*, Nietzsche complained of a "herd" mentality that, as he described it, tends toward "mixing," protects the weak, demands equal rights and "Sympathy with all Sufferers," and where "suffering itself is looked upon by them as something to be *done away* with." As with far-right Libertarianism, Nietzsche was far from proposing the individualized taking of chances. "Socialists," he demurred, have such a "thorough and instinctive hostility to every form of society other than that of the autonomous herd (to the extent even of repudiating the notions of 'master' and 'servant'." Instead of protection, Nietzsche proposed that "the dangerousness of the situation has to be increased enormously" so that a "Will to Life" becomes an "unconditioned Will to Power." Playing the misunderstood genius, he claimed that his "deepest insights" may well appear "as follies, and under certain circumstances as crimes" when they are heard by those who do not believe—as he claims "exoteric and esoteric" peoples have done—"in gradations of rank and not in equality and equal rights." These "insights," Nietzsche proceeded to suggest, "must be almost poison to an entirely different and lower order of human beings" but are nevertheless served up for the exclusive "nourishment and refreshment" of "a higher class of men."[69]

Pharmakon

The absence of a vaccine or known treatments for Covid-19 resulted in an enormous pharmacological rush. It involved efforts to undermine restrictions on drug testing, advertising and prescription guidelines with an epistemological emphasis on intuitive, revelatory knowledge as evidence around a speculative, privatized response to disease transmission. This would ensure a market for untested pharmaceutical products, in particular hydroxychloroquine, to treat Covid-19 symptoms, especially following Donald Trump's endorsement on March 22, 2020. ·

Beyond the political value Trump and similar voices might reap from 'finding' a cure, the pharmacological rush was a boon to companies eager to manage the two greatest uncertainties within the pharmacological circuit of capital: first, the testing of drugs on human subjects to fulfill certification and, second, the creation of demand for a growing consumer market. In that regard, the pandemic presented an opportunity to short-circuit the risk-shifting and allocative mechanisms of contracts intended to protect people from the dangers of powerful pharmaceuticals and their eager developers, from those involved in the clinical trial to the information available at points of prescription and purchase. It undermined whatever methodologies, protocols and advertising restrictions that swing the balance of contract rights from the corporation to test subjects and consumers. And, significantly, it did so by placing the emphasis on intuitive knowledge and the presumably authoritative speech of politicians, rightwing figures and celebrities who declared their optimistic feelings about a drug's efficacy.

The enthusiasm for a marketable pill and other 'magic bullet' solutions was intimately connected with the effort, not exclusive to the US, to bring shutdowns to a close and to circumvent growing demands for the expansion of healthcare and welfare. Yet it also amplified a broader conflict over the balance between, on the one hand, public preventative healthcare and, on the other, the privatized, pharmacological and technolog- ically-intensive treatment of chronic diseases and ill-health. It is precisely this conflict that has resulted in the US being by far the largest retail market for prescription drugs and the most costly healthcare system in the world.[70]

Promoting the use of chloroquine and hydrox- ychloroquine as treatments for Covid-19 in lieu of evidence for the drug's efficacy, Trump announced to a March 22 press conference: "I'm a smart guy." While he admitted that he could not predict whether the drugs would work, he added, "I feel good about it. And we're going to see. You're going to see soon enough." Elsewhere, Trump was insistent that hydroxychloroquine and azithromycin, "taken together, have a real chance to be one of the biggest game changers in the history of medicine." He went on to imply that the Federal Drug Administration had "moved mountains" to speed-up their use, and cited a report on its efficacy that did not rise to any standard for a clinical trial. Asked to comment, the Chief Medical Officer replied: "The president feels optimistic about something, has feelings about it."[71]

Accordingly, Trump ordered the purchase and stockpiling of more than 25 million doses, creating an overnight shortage for those who had been prescribed the drug to treat lupus and malaria. As alarm grew over Trump's promotion of off-label and unproven treatments for Covid-19, a retrospective study found that, of the veterans who had died at US military hospitals after contracting the infection, a greater fraction (by around a third more) of those who had been treated with hydroxychloroquine died than those who had not been administered the drug. Undeterred in the quest for a miracle cure, Trump suggested during a press briefing that industrial bleach might be injected into the lungs so as to clean them, or perhaps UV light—though would later claim he was being sarcastic. Reports suggest he got the idea from a letter he was sent by a group called Genesis II, which styles itself as an evangelical church and is also the producer and distributor of a chlorine bleach product it calls "miracle mineral solution," and which it claims can cure cancer, HIV/AIDS and autism. In mid-May, and having refused to wear a mask or practice physical distancing, Trump claimed to have ordered his doctors to treat him with hydroxychloroquine as a preventative measure—from the same time as it became apparent that a number of White House staffers had tested positive for SARS-CoV-2.

Patriarchal Feelings

Famously, the renowned twentieth-century French philosopher Jacques Derrida made a great deal of Plato's treatment of the *pharmakon* as a metaphor for speech.[72] In the *Phaedrus*, Plato blurs the distinction between well-ordered speech (the *logistikon*) and the *pharmakon*, defined as words which act as an intoxicating or charming potion—much to Derrida's delight. Compared to the Platonism that philosophers have usually extracted from the *Republic*, the *Phaedrus* can seem rather obscure. It suggests a contrast to the more canonically Platonist approach to semantic ambiguity, according to which polysemy imperils the good order of political life, and for which Plato advises the expulsion of the sophists from the city. For Derrida, Plato's ambiguous treatment of the *pharmakon* displaces what he claims is, in the received Platonist system, a rationalist taboo against intuitive knowledge and one that, moreover, threatens the paternal *logos* of the Platonist system.

Contra Derrida, there is no such taboo in Platonist rationalism—not in Plato, whose esoteric geometry is simply less pronounced in the *Republic* than in the *Phaedrus* or *Timaeus*, nor in the writings of subsequent rationalist philosophers (Leibniz, Spinoza, and Descartes) for whom mathematics and geometry were a means of revealing the mind of God. Where intuitionism breaks with rationalism is in the former's treatment of reasoned doubt as corrosive of faith and a hindrance to revelation.

That is, polysemic ambiguity and the embrace of falsehood by patriarchal rulers are clearly not deemed by Plato to constitute a threat to good order or its restoration. To the contrary, for Plato, these are the specified means—the authorized exceptions to and, indeed, the foundation of a preliminary *ratio*—by which the Platonist system permits a turn from the actually-existing republic to dictatorship and tyranny in order to save and perfect the republic. Plato was the first theorist of eugenics. The feelings of the patriarch can serve as substitutes for Plato's *logistikon* because— contrary to the deconstructionists from Derrida to Paul De Man—rationalism (like intuitionism) rests on a metaphysics of *a priori* premises, a seemingly inexplicable but otherwise remarkably consistent feeling and desire for selecting this categorical predicate over that. It is the same logic that, as discussed above, has underpinned exoticist explanations of the virus.

Indeed, this exemption for patriarchal feelings is the most consistent point of Plato's discussion of the *pharmakon*. It is an exemption that Trump extends to himself, as do those around him. In *The Republic*, Plato makes clear that whatever semantic ambiguity he admits is strictly a means of permitting what he regards as politically-useful falsehoods, namely those take "the form of a drug [*pharmakon*]" administered by political rulers for the eugenic benefit of the preservation or reme- dying of the political. He moreover suggests that pharmacological interventions will be required to maintain support for the eugenic regulation of human reproduction, that is: "It will be necessary for the rulers to use many drugs."[73]

Prescribed drugs and lies are not the only things that Plato admits in ruling the *Republic*. In the eighth book, Plato advances a republican defense of despotism. He denounces people moving freely beyond their proper, assigned place, resulting in an excessive freedom where (much to his chagrin) "the purchased slaves, male and female, are no less free than the owners who paid for them."[74] These are the classical metaphysics of the political as a well-defined unit—whose bounded, singular definition is predicated on the exclusion of the enslaved from politics, and the subordination of slaves, women and children in the *oikos*.

Derrida does, eventually, discuss the categorical foundation of Platonism, the link between the *pharmakon* and the political—except that he redescribes it as the psychoanalytic problem of an absent father rather than the political-economic subordination of slaves, women, and children. In treating the threat to a "paternal logos" as if it were the problem of an unattainable origin or lack (the inaccessible father), Derrida limits the deconstruction of the foundational reliance of the *Republic* on the ranked division of *polis* and *oikos*. The trajectory that Derrida offers is far more amenable to the contrarian son, confident in his rejection of the methodology of any "rigorous [explicable] division" in favor of satisfying presumably spontaneous desires, taboo-breaking transgressions, and seemingly mysterious feelings which preserve the ranked Platonist division.

The French microbiologist Didier Raoult has been the prominent medical advocate for the use of hydroxychloroquine and is the source of the study cited by Trump promoting its use. Associated with the political right and described as controversial, in one of his regular, contrarian columns for the conservative magazine *Le Point* he wrote that statins, usually prescribed to lower cholesterol, would be effective in reducing methane production and therefore of assistance in the fight against global warming. He also claimed that it is the need "to be right at all costs that generates scientific work whose veracity is doubtful."[75] Contrary to Raoult, a rigorous meaning of truth is one capable of specifying its conditionality and limits. And so, the question here is who harvests the gains and who shoulders the "costs" when that "scientific work" of drug testing is not only doubtful but actively misleading, damaging and the cause of further illness or deaths. How, then, is risk allocated, including by those contracts that turn patients into research subjects, or those sales in which some are consumers and others are vendors?

Initially, Raoult had undertaken two studies, neither of which fulfilled the criteria of a double-blind or closed-label, randomized clinical trial. Responding to criticisms of those studies, Raoult complained of the "dictatorship of the methodologists."[76] The first of these studies began with 42 patients, only 32 of whom were eventually enrolled in the study. Raoult decided who would be placed in the control group (16 received a placebo) and who would be administered hydroxychloroquine. Information on six of those who were given hydroxychloroquine was "lost in follow-up during the survey because of early cessation of treatment." Furthermore, the researchers decided that, depending on the "clinical presentation" of patients, whether azithromycin would be added to the administration of hydroxychloroquine. Whatever results obtained by such an approach, none of it could plausibly serve as proof of the drug's efficacy.

Released as a preproof by the International Journal of Antimicrobial Agents, the authors concluded that "[d]espite its small sample size our survey shows that hydroxychloroquine treatment is significantly associated with viral load reduction/disappearance in Covid-19 patients and its effect is reinforced by azithromycin."[77] The publishers of the journal, the *International Society of Antimicrobial Chemotherapy*, subsequently released a statement in which they pointed out that "there is currently no large-scale data available on its safety and efficacy" of hydroxychloroquine's use to treat patients with Covid-19.[78] The second study that Raoult participated in as a researcher involved 80 patients who had tested positive for SARS-CoV-2 at the University Hospital Institute Méditerranée Infection. It was also not a closed-label randomized trial. None of the patients were placed in a control group. Those patients who developed pneumonia were given broad-spectrum antibiotics, in addition to a mix of hydroxychloroquine and azithromycin. A non-peer reviewed version of a paper was published online.[79]

Pushing Hydroxychloroquine

Chloroquine, in its generic form, is sold under the brand name of Aralen. It is also available in a different formulation as hydroxychloroquine trading under the brand name Plaquenil. Sanofi, the multinational pharmaceutical company head-quartered in France, owns the trademark for Plaquenil—and, prior to 2020, around a fifth of the global market in prescription drugs, furnishing an estimated annual revenue of over $30 billion and holding well over $100 billion in assets. In France, *Le Monde* reported that in less than a fortnight, 54 cases of cardiac disorders, including four of which were fatal, had been attributed to the use of hydroxychloroquine to treat Covid-19 cases, in some instances used in combination with azithromycin.[80]

In both its chloroquine and hydroxychloro-quine formulations, it is generally approved as a treatment for rheumatoid arthritis, lupus ery-thematosus and malaria. It is not advised as a prescription in complicated cases of malaria, and is ineffective against chloroquine or hydroxychlo-roquine-resistant strains. As for its non-beneficial effects, hydroxychloroquine can cause vomiting and diarrhea, is known to cause eye damage and, in some cases, permanent blindness when used in higher doses, and to cause massive spiking in heart rates, in some cases, lead to heart attacks. Those prescribed the drug for, say, lupus, are required to undergo eye and cardiac tests as a precondition.

Experiments, Trials and Lab Rats

Because there was no standard course of treatments for Covid-19, doctors in hospitals engaged in its extensive off-label use, at times without reporting to health authorities, but invariably as part of a cocktail of drugs administered to patients as a last resort to see if anything might work. In other words, it has been a situation in which it is impossible to accurately discern what, in the event that patients rebounded, had contributed to their recovery or, conversely, if they did not recover or developed additional conditions, what role if any the drug played.

Once politicians and celebrities began touting it as remedy for Covid-19, it became the advertisement for a product in a private and fearful health market—a rush liable to result in shortages for prescribed treatments, fostering the circumvention of its considered administration to patients, and encouraging others to seek it out as if it were a good luck charm against infection. Pharmaceutical companies jockeyed for position, for the authorization of off-label use that eliminated clinical trials as a precondition of sale or administration, for access to both the immense US market in drugs and for test subjects and, not least, around media releases that impacted favorably on their share prices. For instance, while seeking approval for emergency use of its chloroquine product (Resochin), Bayer AG announced that it had donated three million tablets of the drug, which had previously not had access to the vast US retail prescription market.

Hospitalized patients in severe conditions were not, however, the only people being administered with the drug. The US Bureau of Prisons spent around $60,000 on at least one order of hydroxychloroquine sulfate tablets well before there was any evidence for its efficacy. By early April 2020, the Republican governor of Texas announced that 27 SARS-CoV-2 positive residents at one nursing home had been administered hydroxychloroquine in an attempt to "determine whether or not it will be a successful treatment for those patients."[81] The nursing home, called the Resort, had been placed under quarantine. As with prisons, close-quarters had resulted in an enormous increase in the number of infections, the rate of transmission, and the likeliness of a poor prognosis given the age and disabilities of residents. When the governor boasted of the pseudo-clinical trial in a televised address, 83 people, including residents and employees, had tested positive for infection—out of 90 staff and 135 residents, representing around 36 percent of those at the nursing home. Neither the health department nor relatives had been informed of the drug's off-label use. Relatives were not asked to give their consent. Despite this, the governor touted dispensing of the drug as if it were an experiment which would yield an answer to the drug's efficacy, even as that experiment did not meet the standards of any clinical trial.

The campaign for hydroxychloroquine was not restricted to the US—in effect, becoming a global push to relax pharmaceutical regulations. For instance, in Australia, it proceeded as a rather subtle but consequential argument between the medical profession and politicians over the terms of public statements and advertising—and the creation of a demand that would inflate the value and markets of a private pharmaceutical product. The medical professionals on the Health Protection Committee warned that "[a]ppropriate dosage of medications for use in Covid-19 are not yet determined," and went on to add that "there is concern that if used inappropriately, off-label use of medications may cause toxicity and lead to adverse patient outcomes." Unlike the US, Australia prohibits advertising of prescription drugs, and subsidizes the purchase of drugs placed on a registry (the Pharmaceutical Benefits Scheme) as part of its public health system. Leaving aside a discussion of that system's shortcomings, it might nevertheless be noted that the current, conservative Liberal-National government is politically inclined to favor an increasing shift from public to private healthcare. Despite the concerns expressed by doctors, the Australian government added an order of hydroxychloroquine to its national health stockpile, officially to be made available for clinical trials.

Following Derrida, in his history of drug cultures in ancient Athens, Michael Rinella suggests that a "*pharmakon* might be, alternately and simultaneously, a sacrament, remedy, poison, talisman, pigment, cosmetic, perfume, or intoxicant." The very same drug can be remedial, poisonous or sacrificial. It is not, quite, that drugs "lack … a stable essence," as Rinella goes on to suggest.[82] Rather, it is that drugs are biochemicals that become differently active when they come into contact with other biochemical processes: they can be poisonous or remedial at different doses, can have 'side-effects' which are so described because there is never only one discrete effect, and so on. What we know of those processes, or can predict with a degree of confidence, is made possible by the conventions of clinical trials, testing and experiments. There is however no universal human body involving the exact same biochemical processes—a complexity that renders those trials more costly and unpredictable. Moreover, the actual conduct of clinical trials often approximates a sacrifice—of animals and humans—and more cruelly so depending on the conditions under which they are undertaken or allowed to proceed.

For pharmaceutical companies, in addition to the uncertainties of sale, clinical trials represent the largest obstacle between patent and sale. Much of that uncertainty is managed by ensuring the growing desire for a drug through direct or indirect advertisement, including now endorsements by politicians at the rostrum and celebrities on Instagram. It is less that pharmaceutical and biotech companies attempt to recoup the costs of drug development than that the trials are accounted for as the largest variable. Simply put, trials are the uncertain variable in the circuit of pharmacological capital.

The time and cost can be diminished by locating the experiment wherever conditions are

more favorable to the recruitment of subjects who,

without being part of a trial, would have little or no access to any healthcare. Clinical trials are also cheapened through inducements to doctors and regulators. Quarantine confinement can further cheapen the costs of drug trials for the pharmaceutical companies, by displacing the costs of the experiment on to those who have to self-sustain their detainment, or whose close-quarter confinement (in, say, prisons or aged-care facilities) makes it possible to collect data on both disease transmission and the effects of a drug from an immobile population with few exercised rights.

In late March, the Trump administration announced the roll-out of a non-existent vaccine. Dubbed Operation Warp Speed, Moncef Slaoui, a former GlaxoSmithKline executive, was appointed to lead the initiative. Moderna is the first company in the US to proceed to the first of three phases of clinical trial for a vaccine. Slaoui had presumably resigned his position at Moderna to take up the appointment but, per US Securities and Exchange Commission filings, had come into possession of around $10 million of Moderna shares on April 29, 2020.[83]

VAG
ABO
NDS

Liquid Geometries of Value

In a preliminary report released in April 2020 entitled *The Great Economic Lockdown*, the International Monetary Fund predicted that the global economy was expected to sharply contract by around 3 percent in 2020—far worse than the 0.1 percent contraction at the height of the 2007–09 global financial crisis. A second outbreak in 2021, the report suggested, would push GDP nearly 5 percent below the 2020 baseline, effectively canceling its projections of a relatively swift economic recovery. Their worst-case scenario was of a longer outbreak in 2020 followed by a resurgence of the virus the following year and a drop of global output of around 8 percent below the base scenario—resulting in a sharp contraction of GDP, a two-year economic crisis and skyrocketing government debt.[84]

Remarkably, this was the first time that the IMF has integrated epidemiologists in its economic modeling, leading to the conclusion that, while the "great lockdown" had prompted a decline in GDP, the failure to disrupt disease transmission will worsen the economic impact. There is a long history of using biological contagion as a trope to discuss the physics of economic and financial crises—one I have discussed at length in *Contract*

& Contagion. But by arguing that the severity of the economic crisis will be determined by how effectively disease transmission is handled, the report cuts across the grain of more conventional and metaphorical accounts that tend to blur the distinction. For economic nationalists, lately enjoying a renewed popularity, the travel bans, quarantines and lockdowns serve as proof of the argument that all flows are conduits of economic dis-ease. Those who claim that there is a stark choice to be made between reopening the economy and halting disease transmission likewise treat all flows between solids as the same.

This is not to suggest that the IMF has proposed a better path. It is to suggest that the range of proposed economic policies from the IMF and other organizations are, despite consequential differences between them, turned toward answering much the same questions: how to satisfy growing demand for liquidity (cash to meet short-term obligations), and in such a way that preserves the presumably solid shapes and obligations of national economic growth post-Covid-19. It remains an open question whether this converts into a ferocious post-crisis austerity, or increasing central bank intervention coupled with progressive taxation reform or, as proponents of modern monetary theory argue, the suspension of debt obligations through the printing of money. The direction of policy has already been partially shaped by central banks lowering of interest rates and issuance of government bonds, the structuring of so-called stimulus packages involving discount windows, commercial rent and mortgage

deferments and conditions placed on any temporary expansions in health and welfare spending.
Nevertheless, the implications of these different
approaches rest on their respective handling of
the analogy drawn between national economies
and households—which will be briefly discussed
further below.

There are, however, other ways of approaching the issues of liquidity and productivity than
through a national economic lens. To that end,
what follows is a brief discussion of catastrophe
bonds and the supply-chain of personal protective
equipment—the point of which is to foreground
the role of insurance and risk management
in conditioning liquidity and creating shortages in the supply of goods. It is not the world
imagined by economic policy debates insofar as
those approaches draw firm distinctions between
markets and states, global and national organization, or finance and economics. But it is a
discussion that highlights the significance, *contra*
economic naturalism, of a historical understanding of use-values and needs. It is also, implicitly,
a rejection of the lifeboat ethics of economic
nationalism.[85] What matters during a disaster is
whether needs are met, and in capitalism that
requires liquid cash.

Pandemic Bonds

In mid-2016, the World Bank announced its
intention to establish a Pandemic Emergency
Financing Facility. What the PEFF has done, in
short, is freeze the liquidity of foreign aid and

disaster relief by financializing the epidemiological curve. The financial instrument, a three-year pandemic bond, was launched on June 28, 2017—scheduled therefore to mature on June 28, 2020. The World Bank is not the only organization to have issued a pandemic bond. The first catastrophe bond was released by the reinsurer Hanover Re in 1994—in the wake of Hurricane Andrew in 1992 which led to $22 billion in insurance claims and widespread filings for bankruptcy by insurers.

From the perspective of the insurance industry, catastrophe bonds represent an effort by reinsurers (large firms who in effect act as wholesale insurers to protect the consumer insurance industry) to mitigate against the risk of high financial losses and insolvency in the event of a catastrophe. They do so by shifting the risk of a sudden escalation in numerous claims to capital markets: in the hypothetical event of a catastrophe, the bonds would furnish short-term liquidity, with cash raised from the creation of a short-term speculative market on the possibilities of a catastrophic event occurring for a defined period of time. It would ward off insurance company bankruptcy in the event of a cascade of claims. Traded as bonds and swaps outside of centralized exchanges such as the New York Stock Exchange, for large institutional investors such as pension and hedge funds, they represent a time-limited, high-risk, and potentially high-return wager—one that furnishes a different set of probabilities within a portfolio to other wagers and therefore acts as an exotic hedge. The risk that investors run is that they lose their investment if there is a pandemic event during the time of the bond. The importance for pension fund investors is that it acts as a hedge between calls on pension funds (the end of work) and calls on life and other insurance.

From the perspective of governments, the catastrophe bond (cat bond for short) promises, on the one hand, to finance an emergency response or pay for a conditioned economic stimulus and, on the other hand, for those governments who pay interest on the bond, promises a reduction in foreign disaster relief funding. Significantly, it offers the prospect of doing so under regular conditions of austerity. It theoretically offers a timely injection of liquid cash at the time of an emergency without meanwhile disrupting the rule of austerity by expanding healthcare or welfare, even while the latter are important preventative measures. Moreover, it incorporates the logic of financial yield within state policy—including by converting catastrophic events (or the imagination of them) into a financial asset, because it can be weighed against (hedged) or bundled with other similarly financialized assets (securitized). In this sense, catastrophe bonds are of a piece with social impact or social benefit bonds, which transform the governance of welfare and social policy along the same lines.[86]

As with impact bonds, not all catastrophe bonds have the same conditions and implications. For instance, Swiss Re's extreme mortality bonds, or Vita Capital, is principally a method of risk-shifting between pension funds, reinsurers and insurers, payable in the event that any catastrophe leads to deaths exceeding 130 percent of a historical baseline (formulated from mortality rates in the US, UK, France, and Switzerland). In the current pandemic it is unclear whether and how this, or similar metrics, may have played a role in the accounting of deaths and their causes during the pandemic. What is nevertheless likely is that this added to the pressure on the UK government to include deaths outside of hospitals in its figures. The implications of Vita Capital's structure are related to the payout of life insurance claims, and any sudden, cumulative effects on the solvency of insurers in the event of an extreme mortality event.

The World Bank's pandemic bond, by contrast, specifically stipulated attribution of deaths to a pandemic as the trigger for a payout to governments ranked low on the GDP per population scale. It moreover assumes that the reported case count of infections and attributions of death certifications are accurate.

Structured by Swiss Re and Munich Re, and managed by Munich Re and GC Securities, the World Bank's pandemic bond represents the restructuring of inter-government foreign aid and disaster relief through a merger of insurance, financial markets and governments. In this case, the Japanese, Australian, and German governments (the PEFF's steering committee) pay the interest on the pandemic bond to investors. Presumably this is in lieu of paying foreign aid directly. By contrast, governments eligible for financing by the PEFF in the event of a pandemic are those ranked low on measures of GDP per capita. Perhaps in other words, rather than use aid dollars to directly fund increased capacity to prevent or mitigate future disasters, or suppress the spread of a pandemic from the point of an outbreak, those funds are now dedicated to purchasing an insurance policy by which populations will benefit only if they first die in sufficient numbers.

Yet despite claims that it would furnish liquidity, the complexity of the PEFF's trigger has rendered it ineffective as a means of preventing the spread of a highly-contagious respiratory infection. The fund did not pay out during the 2018 Ebola epidemic, which killed more than 2,000 people in the Democratic Republic of Congo. And it was some four months into the SARS-CoV-2 pandemic before it triggered any payouts.

In order for eligible governments to receive a payment, a period of at least twelve weeks would have to elapse from the time of an initial outbreak—set in this case by the WHO from December 31, 2019 (and not, as some have claimed, set by the date on which the WHO declared the existence of a pandemic). The outbreak would have to occur in at least two countries eligible for International Development Association or International Bank for Reconstruction and Development funds, with each of these countries having at least 20 confirmed deaths. Moreover, the number of deaths and cases attributable to the pandemic would have to be expressed as a defined point on an exponential or epidemiological curve of confirmed cases and attributed deaths. Additionally, regional outbreaks affecting two to seven eligible countries would trigger payments in three stages as the number of total confirmed deaths increased, and global outbreaks affecting eight or more countries would also activate payouts in three stages but provide access to higher funding levels at the first two triggers.

On April 9, 2020 the World Bank issued a statement announcing that the conditions for payouts had not been met. "Some of the activation criteria," the statement read, "such as outbreak size and spread across borders, have already been met," but not "an exponential growth rate" in the low-income economies of East Asia and the Pacific and the middle-income economies in Latin America and the Caribbean, "as calculated by the third-party calculation agent (AIR Worldwide)."[87] The SARS-CoV-2 pandemic had not, according to the risk analytics firm AIR, yet reached the specified standard of an eligible event.

Since the exponential growth chart had continued to trend upwards, by April 27, the World Bank announced that funding packages ranging from $1 to $15 million per country would be distributed, depending on the extent to which those countries had been "classified as fragile or conflict-affected." It also stated that the funds would assist governments in the purchase of "essential and critical life-saving medical equipment, personal protective equipment, therapeutics and medicine, as well as support for health workers on the frontlines of the crisis."

It is not yet clear what situating the cat bond's short tail at an upper point in the arc of the epidemiological curve meant for investors. What is nevertheless clear is that the liquidity promised by the PEFF was not so liquid after all. It froze the movement of money with which to either make or purchase the equipment necessary to stem the transmission of disease, or boost healthcare capacity, or facilitate relatively low-cost physical interventions (such as public health information about handwashing, or masks) earlier in the course of the pandemic. That is, the pandemic bond has resulted in the World Bank, government sponsors and investors watching the spread of an infectious disease and increasing numbers of dead in poor countries before taking steps that might have halted that spread or reduced the number of deaths. Many things remain unclear: whether those purchases of, say, PPE are conditioned, what precise impact the delay has had on efforts to stem the transmission of the disease or any increase in mortality rates, whether the funds are sufficient or, indeed, whether having a small amount of cash and limits on availability makes any difference.

Before turning to a discussion of the supply-chain of PPE and explanations of its failures, it nevertheless bears underlining a point in this instance: the pandemic bond was a means of restructuring aid packages that, awkwardly, sought to incorporate epidemiological metrics into a financial instrument, one traded outside of central exchanges, and purportedly as a means of global health governance and pandemic response funding. States were not outside of this complex, but government foreign aid was transformed by it nevertheless. Nor were measures of GDP—in this case serving as the principal ranked distinction between sponsors of the pandemic bond and its recipients. GDP is not a measure of some eternal idea of productivity but, rather, the statistical aggregate of realized sales of commodities within and at a nation's borders. The realization of exchange-value in a defined market is the terminus of liquid cash.

Supply-Chain Logistics

In 2018, the global market in PPE was estimated to be around $2.5 billion. Before the pandemic, most of the world's PPE (masks, protective suits, goggles and gowns) were produced in and exported from China, followed by Germany and the US. The supply-chain was marked by highly concentrated regional distribution markets (of the Americas, Europe, and Asia), though is somewhat different in the case of specific equipment. The largest proportion of surgical gloves, for instance, are exported from Malaysia, followed by Thailand and China. Principal vendors within European markets are based in Belgium, France, Germany, Italy, the Netherlands and Poland. Most purchases of PPE produced in China (and of gloves in Malaysia) were made by buyers in the US, and US companies were the largest distributors in North and South American markets. (By way of comparison with related products, South Korea and India are the most significant manufacturers of medicines and vaccines, and Singapore is a key hub of pharmaceutical companies.)[88]

Depicting supply-chains as spatial links between countries and regions makes sense for a few reasons, but not without qualification. Contrary to a resurgent economic nationalism, the manufacture of a PPE device in a given country does not mean that needs for that device within that country are or will be met. Nor does it mean that a manufacturing process operates independently of machinery and materials sourced from elsewhere. Further, a growth in national manufacturing can result in a growth in the GDP but not in wages or the distribution of wealth. It might not mean that production will involve work which is paid well below the national average as a result of, say, the gendered labor conditions in garment manufacturing or the tax arrangements of trade zones. The ideal predicate of economic nationalism—analogous to separate, economically self-sufficient households—has never existed. But its myth has obscured divisions within and between economies, including by treating the appropriation of nature as continuous with that division (as with extraction and unpaid or low-paid labor).

This is not to suggest that country-based diagrams of supply-chains are irrelevant. Far from it. They can point to distinct conditions of materials processing and manufacture (such as labor and environmental laws); discrete taxation, import and export arrangements; make it possible to estimate the relative costs of production, imports and exports based on the relative value of currencies; implicitly illustrate discrete or regional systems of PPE certification (as with certification guidelines within the European market). Supply-chains are slung together through the use of auditing, certification and management systems, and marked by competing trademarks and contracts. Stretching across national spaces, some of the largest companies involved in surgical and N-series masks are 3M, Cartel Healthcare, Kwalitex Healthcare, and Magnum Health. Some of the largest companies involved in the trademarked manufacture of A-level hazmat suits are DuPont, 3M, Dragerwerk AG, and Halyard Health. The legal bundling and structuring of trademarks, headquartering, regional offices, subsidiaries, and supply and distributor contracts are ways of handling the differences between jurisdictions so as to optimize profits.

Indeed, more than a geographic or spatial diagram, supply-chains are the corollary of Coasean redescriptions of the firm as a bundle of contracts. Except that it is a complex bundle of contracts in an uncertain sequence and in motion, at once fragile and entrepreneurial, facilitating the assembly and movements of a commodity to its final destination in sale. It is one in which different sets of laws and standards, and the markets and prices to which they give rise, present opportunities for arbitrage, risk-shifting and, as occurred during the pandemic, the auctioning of inventory outside manufacturing plants or at airports. To view supply-chains as the result of globalization is to miss the point and difference that borders make to profitability—in the detail, an archipelago of labor and migration policies, financing, trade agreements and prohibitions, processing zones, and certification.

That is, supply-chains were never one pipeline from materials to construction to market. The pandemic rendered them more opaque than they had ever been. While the practice of just-in-time

inventories shifted the balance of power in contracts downstream to vendors and trademark
holders, production shutdowns as a result of quarantines and temporary export bans during the
pandemic precipitated a scramble that resulted
in auctions of materials and inventories further
upstream. Where the trades were auctions, the
US dollar tended to prevail by dint of its relative
value. As for stockpiling by governments, it
has been organized less as a means of responding to increased demand during an emergency
than a (theoretical) method of smoothing price
shocks. Even then, in notable instances, it neither
decreased the price nor increased the supply of
critical PPE during the pandemic. Globally, the
WHO estimated a six-fold increase in the price
of surgical masks, three-fold for respirators and
a doubling in the price of gowns during the
pandemic. The problem, bluntly put, is that PPE
is a commodity.

This was starkly illustrated by the emergency
supply-chain unit in the US federal government's
taskforce—headed up by Vice-President Mike
Pence, officially run by Admiral John Polowczyk
and, prominently, influenced by Jared Kushner.
It operated largely in secrecy, facilitating the
expansion of favored companies and their rapidly
growing markets in PPE, test-kits and ventilators.
It competed with both states within the US and
other governments over contracts and purchase
orders—including, infamously, in the last minute,
tense standoffs on airport tarmacs. It also
contracted directly with some of the largest corporations, such as the petrochemical giant, DuPont.

They dubbed this Project Airbridge—presumably as an allusion to the 1948–49 Berlin Airlift of the Cold War when the US-led allied forces air-dropped supplies in West Berlin to break a Soviet blockade of goods destined for the then-divided German capital. The name is a reminder that the history of logistics begins in a nineteenth century theory of operational warfare—as is the appointment of Polowczyk from a background in military logistics and defense contracting. The logistical theory of warfare is concerned with uncertainty over the continuous transmission of energy. It describes a decisive conflict as the effective application of force on critical points. It is an operational or 'geometric' theory of war steeped in frontier and colonial warfare.[89] In the case of Project Airbridge, it underlines the distinctiveness of capitalist definitions of uncertainty and risk as questions about the uncertainty of realized profits and the risks of a breakdown in the circuit of capital. A key risk is the uncertain leap between the production of a commodity and its realization of value in its sale—one that has long resulted in endogenous capitalist crises.

In mainstream media explanations of PPE shortages and descriptions of chaotic organization, a great deal of emphasis has been accorded to the ousting of the biosecurity and pandemic preparedness units of previous administrations with Trump's appointment of the notorious hawk John Bolton as national security advisor in 2017. Some of these explanations are due to conflicts within various Republican factions and with prior administrations. But this perspective obscures, for instance, the grotesque response to Hurricane Katrina. However, the duration between the Trump administration's confident assertions that the pandemic was under control through travel bans and the eventual establishment of the task-force can also be read as a moment in which the object of speculation expanded: from the political value of xenophobic travel bans to encompass estimates on the political and financial value of PPE, test-kits, and ventilator markets. As with the CDC's decision to spend crucial weeks developing its own test-kits (that turned out to be faulty) rather than import WHO-approved test-kits from Germany, the administration's early mercantilist impulse expanded to facilitating the monopolization of US markets.

Previous administrations were similarly inclined to venture into highly speculative treatments of catastrophe and national security. In the recently-released email threads of the so-called Red Dawn group of March 11–12, Tom Bossert—who a year earlier had been Trump's Senior Director for Preparedness Policy—asked whether anyone could "justify the European travel restrictions, scientifically? Seriously, is there any benefit? I don't see it, but I'm hoping there is something I don't know." James Lawler—an infectious-disease doctor at the University of Nebraska, and member of the Homeland and National Security councils during the Bush and Obama presidencies—replied, "Fuck no. This is the absolute wrong move." They were responding, at the time privately, to Trump's major announcement on March 11 that travel bans would be extended, which the president had described as "the most aggressive and comprehensive effort to confront a foreign virus in modern history." It clearly was not. When Trump delivered the televised address, there were already around 1,200 confirmed cases of SARS-CoV-2 infections in the US, including 36 deaths. Almost a month later on April 13, there would be 584,862 confirmed cases, and 23,555 people had died. Yet what Lawler adds to the same email conversation illustrates the extent to which previous White House administrations were similarly inclined to speculation and a reliance on intuited assumptions. As Lawler went on to say in this same conversation, the Trump administration was making decisions "based on intuition," not "what the instruments tell them." It was, in his view, a repetition of "every misstep leaders initially made in table-tops at the outset of pandemic planning in 2006." The table-top exercise is an extension of the logistical approach to war as "the art of moving armies" and "making war on the map."[90] Whatever the benefits of the table-top—in scenario-planning, it is a procedural review used to identify the ways in which the simulation of a disaster does not approximate an actual disaster—what these remarks make clear is that a shift did take place between the fictive imagination of a pandemic and the Trump administration's realization that PPE was a growing market in which it could become a key intermediary in demand allocation and purchasing. We will only know in retrospect whether this was so as to mediate to the disbursement of influence and favors, to engage in self-dealing and for undisclosed financial benefit (as the Trump business has been indicted on before), or as a means of withholding equipment such that, in effect, it functioned as a *de facto* eugenic policy, by offering some the means of protection and not others.

Nevertheless, at the center of Project Airbridge was an agreement, according to which the federal government would underwrite or pay for the transportation costs in the supply-chain in exchange for the purchase and sale of 60 percent of the inventory. The allocation was a 40-40-20 split: 20 percent would be purchased by the federal government and placed in the Strategic National Stockpile; the taskforce would decide which buyers would have access to an additional 40 percent; and the companies would decide what to do with the remaining 40 percent.

In January, DuPont increased production of PPE, including suits which it usually sells for around $5 to hospitals. The DuPont plant in Richmond, Virginia produces the patented material, Tyvek, which it ships to Vietnam where the suits are made. It would usually take three months between the shipping of materials to Vietnam, manufacture in Vietnam, and the return of the finished products to be sold in US markets. The federal government offered to reduce the transport time to ten days by paying for chartered flights (mostly from Federal Express). There were other, less public intermediaries. The large supply company, W.W. Grainger Inc., bought the suits from DuPont and sold them on to the US federal government at almost double what it had paid DuPont.[91] In March, Grainger was sent a warning by the Wisconsin Department of Consumer Protection Agency over reports that it had increased the price of N95 masks by 600 percent.[92]

The power of the US government to intervene in global sales of PPE—and, in concert with large manufacturers, reshape both supply-chains and markets—is a function of the relative value of the US dollar that has allowed it to run up massive debts. It is that exceptional capacity that the US federal government wielded to outbid other buyers and governments, including US state governments. Whether, in the final tally, most global trades in PPE will have been settled in US dollars will be an index of whether that capacity remains intact. At the same time, some governments imposed temporary export bans on PPE and, often the same governments at other moments, facilitated a growing export industry. Trump publicly thanked "our friends in Vietnam" for some 450,000 hazmat suits. Manufacturing in Vietnam (and Bangladesh) had expanded somewhat prior to the pandemic as a result of companies with US sales markets shifting their supply contracts from China to Vietnam in an attempt to avoid US tariffs recently imposed on imports from China. Meanwhile, a Vietnamese billionaire donated masks and other PPE equipment to the Philippines government. Global economic and political blocs were being refashioned and affirmed through PPE supply-chains—increasingly described as the exercise of so-called soft power through prominently donated supplies and as the consolidation of (emerging) trade networks and agreements.

Yet this is also a remarkable illustration of the complexity of risk-shifting. That is, firstly, the externalization of the dangers of a given system of production as socialized pollution and, secondly, the commercialization of healthcare devices for mitigating against the impact of diseases whose severity has been linked to other, so-called underlying diseases associated with that pollution.

Products such as Lycra, Tyvek, and Teflon elevated DuPont—the nineteenth-century gunpowder mill that had enjoyed a virtual monopoly on gunpowder during the US Civil War—into today's petrochemical giant. When DuPont decided to scale up its production of Tyvek, it had barely emerged from a 15-year-long class-action lawsuit over its use of a chemical compound called perfluorooctanoic acid (PFOA, or C8) in the making of Teflon—which had cost the company around a billion dollars over some years. DuPont began using PFOA to make Teflon and related polymers in 1951. Some eight companies in the US have been cited as responsible for PFOA pollution, including 3M—another large manufacturer of PPE, which produced PFOA as an industrial chemical and sold it to DuPont. PFOA has been in existence for less than a century, but by 1978, 3M detected amounts in its workers' blood, and DuPont was privately expressing concerns about toxic effects at its Washington plant. Based on a study in 2003–04, the CDC found that PFOA exposure was ubiquitous throughout the general US population.

From documents disclosed at trial, researchers at the National Bureau of Economic Research asked whether pollution was viewed as value-maximizing by DuPont and concluded that, yes, "under reasonable probabilities of detection, polluting was [seen as] ex-ante optimal from the company's perspective, even if the cost of preventing pollution was lower than the cost of the health damages produced."[93] A separate, epidemiological study revealed a strong correlation between PFOA and higher incidences of a range of cancers, high cholesterol, thyroid disease, and pregnancy-induced hypertension.[94] Many of those diseases have been identified as worsening the impact of a SARS-CoV-2 infection.

The same companies can occupy contradictory positions from the perspective of health because financial losses can be hedged against financial gains. That PPE has become such an important commodity is nevertheless a reminder that the use-value of a commodity serves, for capital, as a warranty on the realization of that commodity's exchange-value. The shunting of risks can, however, operate just as easily in a nominally public health system that, in practice, is a conglomeration of public and private contracts.

As in the US, the UK government was initially publicly confident, in this case that its stockpile of PPE was sufficient to handle the outbreak of a novel coronavirus. It nevertheless similarly resulted in shortages. On February 11, the chief commercial officer at the Department of Health and Social Care issued a letter reassuring staff that the National Health Service (NHS) "and wider health system are extremely well prepared for these types of outbreaks." Except that it appears no one had ever raised, in previous scenario planning exercises, "the possibility of a non-flu pandemic."[95] The bulk of the existing pandemic stockpile was purchased for an influenza outbreak, not the fluid-repellent gowns and shields required to interrupt the transmission of SARS-CoV-2, particularly that which occurs between patients and healthworkers during aerosol-generating procedures. Throughout March and April, contradictory guidelines were issued to NHS staff regarding the appropriate PPE for certain procedures and, it seems, there was no one on the government's principal taskforce who knew or was capable of explaining the difference between influenza and coronavirus transmission. Due to the increasing number of deaths of healthworkers, growing anxiety about adequate PPE supplies, and increasingly gaslit by the government's and conservative media discourse of heroic self-sacrifice, by the end of April the NHS was on the brink of exhaustion, trapped in the daily accumulation of moments during which healthworkers were forced to wonder whether treating a patient might result in their own death.

VĀG
ABO
NDS

Economy and Infrastructure

Conventional understandings of infrastructure
are theories of movement or circulation premised
on a theory of forms—as in the implied distinction
between critical infrastructure and the national
economy utilized by the Centers for Disease
Control. The CDC defined "critical infrastructure during COVID-19" as 16 sectors involving
"assets, systems, and networks, whether physical
or virtual, [that] are considered so vital to the
United States that their incapacitation or destruction would have a debilitating effect on security,
national economic security, national public health
or safety." That infrastructure includes commu-
nications, "critical manufacturing," transport,
energy, food and agriculture, healthcare, water
and wastewater systems, defense and "government facilities."[96]

Their criticality consists of their being deemed
essential to securing the national economy and
health of a defined public. With the insertion
of "critical manufacturing," food, agriculture,
healthcare, defense and the implicit inclusion of
prisons and immigration detention among "government facilities," infrastructure comes to mean
both that which is both necessary to the continuous transmission of energy, broadly described,

and the preservation of the economy. It is not a description of infrastructure which existed prior to the late twentieth century. But it is one that is distinguished from the ideal economic units of national economy and household—and, in that sense, represents a recent perturbation within and retrieval of an old diagram. In philosophical terms, this view of infrastructure is the perspective of a troubled Platonism. That is, while it mystifies the contested history of property laws and systems of appropriation that give rise to the formation of private property at various categorical scales (household, corporation, nation), it is nevertheless preoccupied with the problem of how movement might be converted into an orderly circulation and accumulation.

On one hand, the division between actual households—those reliant on liquid cash (wages or social incomes) with which to live, pay rent or mortgages and those households in which the home is an asset—is often elided in the metaphorical analogy drawn between national economies and households. That division is highly gendered and racialized. For instance, according to census figures on housing ownership in the US in 2019, over 70 percent of white people owned their own home, above the national average of around 65 percent, and as compared with between 41 and 56 percent of non-whites. The conditions of lending and debt are similarly patterned and heighten these divisions. Moreover, the assumption that political rights and citizenship are varieties of inherited entitlement rests on a naturalized analogy between private property law and political representation.

On the other hand, the lockdowns foregrounded the division between the entitled *demos* and working populations. On March 19, the US government issued guidelines stipulating that those working "in a critical infrastructure industry ... such as healthcare services and pharmaceutical and food supply" and instructing them: "you have a special responsibility to maintain" your "normal work schedule."[97] The latter resulted, for instance, in an informal system of letters from employers temporarily putting a hold on deportations of undocumented workers in agriculture, food processing and related "critical infrastructure."

By May 3 in the US, overall cases of infection soared past 1.1 million, and well over 67,000 people had died. The largest clusters of infection were in prisons, food processing plants and aboard ships: Marion Correctional Institution, Pickaway Correctional Institution, Smithfield Foods pork processing facility, Trousdale Turner Correctional Center, the USS *Theodore Roosevelt*, Cook County jail, Cummins Unit prison and the Tyson Foods meatpacking plant. One of the largest outbreaks, at the Smithfield pork factory in Sioux Falls, South Dakota, was worked predominantly by people who had arrived on refugee visas. The largest clusters of deaths were in assisted living facilities. One study of available data in the US showed that aged care facilities with a significant number of Black and Latinx residents have been twice as likely to be hit by the coronavirus as those where the population is overwhelmingly white.[98]

Throughout the US, prison labor was used to produce disinfectants and protective equipment, launder hospital attire, manufacture protective equipment and dig mass graves.[99] Outside of these clusters in prisons and food processing, the pattern was much the same. A third of Louisiana residents are Black, though almost 60 percent of those who have died from the disease are Black; in Michigan: less than 15 percent, but around 40 percent of deaths; in South Dakota: less than 20 percent, but just under 70 percent of deaths; in Washington, a Black person was more than twice as likely to die from Covid-19 as a white person. The pattern in the UK is similar. Black and Brown people are around 13 percent of the population, but around a third of patients admitted to critical care units. They also represent more than 70 percent of healthworkers who have died—whose distinct circumstances of work, involving repeated contact with infections with inadequate protective equipment, remains an enormous factor.

Money and Debt

Money and debt, understood as a circulating medium of value and obligation, and the metrics of "the wealth of nations," are pivotal to the idea of distinct economic categories—and a key variable in the gathering storm of post-pandemic economic policy and the uncertainties of the swerve.

Briefly, economic liberalism, in its Smithian version, treats government regulation as an infringement on the moral economic (and patriarchal) management of private households (or, by extension, other private contracts such as those of the corporation). For Adam Smith, measures of the "wealth of nations"—such as the twentieth-century's GDP, based on Smith's proposal for such a metric—are meant to serve as a guide to that management by self-regulating (patriarchal) households. This is the crux of the meaning of economic liberalism—not the absence of regulation but its relegation to intimate, private laws, norms, and contracts. Because actual households are not those envisaged by classical political-economy, in practice the liberal tenet of *laissez faire* has largely served to displace risks onto actual households and therefore both relies on and exacerbates the disparities of wealth and power between and within households— including whether the principal source of income is liquid cash incomes (wages and social incomes) or assets (capital). More conservative approaches than those of Smith, such as those of Malthus and Karl Polanyi, are similarly disposed—albeit with a more explicit conflation of home and nation. For Polanyi, economics policy was explicitly understood as "householding."[100]

There are numerous, looming proposals for handling any presumed debts arising from the injections of liquidity during the pandemic. Of these, modern monetary theory has become one of the most prominent but received far less scrutiny because it is assumed to be outside the conventional understandings of debt. Modern monetarism has incorporated the insight that economies are not analogous to households because the latter do not print money—or, as the US investment banker Daniel Alpert put it in an article on pandemic-induced national debts: "The US, the UK, and Japan print their own currencies and issue their national debt only in their own currencies."[101] This is a distortion whose principal effect is to obscure relations of exploitation. Nation-states do not print money (of unchanging value) so much as issue denominated currencies of relatively-ranked values—or the relatively-valued expectations implicit in government bonds where those have been used to fund stimulus packages. The US in particular has been able to run up debt without consequence because it has held the *de facto* global currency in which a large proportion of trade and debts are reckoned and settled. In August 2019, almost 62 percent of global foreign exchange reserves were in US dollars.

Having emerged from Polanyian economics, modern monetarism reframes the issue of debt as the interiorized, national accounting of obligations between the owners of property—not the exploitative relations that give rise to surplus value and therefore capital, nor the divisions between and within actual households or economies. In doing so, it mystifies the hierarchies within national economies and between them because its principal assumption is that 'the economy,' unlike money, is presumably natural and economies ought to—apparently like households or perhaps plantations—function principally through 'gifted' or bound labor. It renders the Polanyian dichotomy (between the artifice of money and national economic production deemed natural) into the

assumption that money is a neutral medium of
exchange—or, the suggestion that it could be, if
only markets were regulated by states, understood
as analogous to private estates, and the price of
money (i.e. interest rates) in a given currency for
the owners of capital was set at around zero.

Except that the distinction between states and
markets, no less than that drawn between economies and money, does not survive the barest
scrutiny. The GDP is not an indicator of general
social and economic well-being. GDP per capita
tells us nothing about the distribution of wealth
within a country. On the contrary, GDP is the statistical aggregate of realized sales of commodities
within and at a nation's borders. Far from representing something called 'the real economy' or
'real productivity,' the GDP is no less an index of
market activity than are Wall Street stock prices.

As for modern monetarism: in treating national
productivity as an assumed good, the GDP as its
normative index, and household and national
debt as contiguous synonyms for tyranny (or 'debt
slavery'), it rehearses the categorical premises
of economic liberalism while, at the same time,
impeding a radical understanding of debt that
might challenge the hierarchical (gendered and
racial) logic of economic sacrifice rendered at
once invisible and necessary by those presumably
homogeneous categories.

Postpandem Contracts

The principal distinction between modern monetarism and other monetarist or post-Keynesian

approaches is the expectation of the former that the money currently being borrowed for "huge coronavirus bailouts" will not have to be repaid, because inflation has been suppressed and, if not completely, "a central bank can print enough money to cover the interest on government debt for as long as it likes."[102]

Firstly, the key way in which inflation has been subdued since the late 1980s is through the suppression of wage and social income growth—and through means which have widened the division between those reliant on liquid cash in order to survive and those who own (heritable) property or assets. By the terms of population and political contract theory discussed above, this is a political-economic distinction between working populations and an entitled *demos*—though it is one that is drawn far more neatly and differently in political representation than it is in economic policies and practices. Not least among these methods has been the expansion of precarious wage contracts beyond their Fordist margins, migration policies that deliver workers with fewer political and economic rights, the borders which make arbitrage possible through the tangled lines of global supply-chains, the entrenchment of workfare and prison labor, and the growth of permanent or unpayable debt.[103] These brought about conditions of near-full employment while preserving labor discipline and wage restraint. Put another way, it was achieved by superseding the Kaleckian dilemma but, at the same time, it invalidated the moral economic claim that waged work is a remedy to poverty.[104]

Secondly, and on the other side of these equa-
tions, in addition to systems of permanent debt
traded as an asset, an enormous portion of
income liquidity was captured by the massive
growth of pension funds and consumption or
other indirect taxes since the 1980s. Estimated
at around $44 trillion (USD) in 2018, pension
funds are arguably the largest single source of
investments in bonds and securities—including the World Bank's pandemic bond and other
catastrophe bonds, and government bonds issued
to finance the bailouts. Together, these funds, debt
obligations and the expectation that inflation has
been suppressed, financed and underwrote the
"huge coronavirus bailouts." The vast portion of
those "bailouts" furnished commercial loans or
discount windows—to affray declining commerce
during the partial shutdown and, indirectly, as a
means to supplement stock-market declines (which
are usually, and in effect, low-interest loans to
corporations). Government debt accrued as a consequence of those "bailouts" only shows up on the
asset side of the national ledger (as modern monetarists and post-Keynesians contend) inasmuch
as it is assumed those obligations will be settled
in some presumably isolated national currency,
there are no imports or exports of products or
materials involved, and because, for the most part,
they involve the expectation that governments will
effectively manage capitalism within and at their
borders, as represented by the GDP—and will
continue to do so after the pandemic in much the
same fashion as they did before.

Thirdly, in treating national debt as exemplary and—mostly as a metaphor for the purposes of political affiliation—as implicitly continuous with household and company ownership and debt, such approaches ignore all the ways in which not all debts are the same. Indeed, some debts are rendered as default or natural by that nationalist exemplification—including that which is understood as a debt of labor owed. In the history of capitalism, this idea of labor as an unpaid debt was explicitly enshrined in such things as fugitive slave laws and tenets of legal personhood and, more implicitly, in theologies of sin and salvation. Indeed, US federal powers of detention and deportation were assembled on the legal precedents of the Fugitive Slave Acts—the defined "due process" of seizing property. In the context of post-pandemic reckonings, the idea of labor as an unpaid debt presents itself as that of a heroic sacrifice remunerated by applause, re-employment of furloughed or quarantined workers under reduced conditions and a narrower labor market and, not least, as arguments for the permanent expansion of immigration restrictions, policing and surveillance. In those instances where it is impossible to avoid dealing with labor as an unpredictable, troublesome variable in reckonings of national debt, there are already suggestions to handle this through corporatism.

Briefly, corporatism is where unions are directly incorporated into systems of capitalist governance (including in government policy apparatuses or on corporate and pension fund boards) and, less directly, invested with the idea of economic nationalism (imbued with a heightened interest in regulating both the cross-border movements of workers and strike action). While political corporatism has its historical origins in organicist descriptions of the nation (as described above), contemporary corporatism treats that biological metaphor as implicit in an effort to suppress the possibilities of inflation in wage and social incomes. Either way, corporatism preserves the categorical division of liquid incomes and capital by treating their apparent representatives as partners in a political-economic contract whose terms they enforce.

There is no immediate policy or political route out of this impasse because politics—at least that which is understood as the subordination or taming of economic conflict—creates its terms and limits. The electoral losses of the campaigns within UK Labour and the US Democrats, as represented by Jeremy Corbyn and Bernie Sanders respectively, did not create that impasse. But they were symptomatic of a dilemma that cannot be resolved within politics, particularly as the predicate of national representation distorts its stakes and conditions. On the one hand, the political right has prioritized limits on citizenship and the franchise and, therefore, on lawmaking and definitions of legalized violence. On the other, ongoing debates on the left over migration, the connection of class politics to those of race and gender, and of empire to colonialism are the political refraction of conflicts over where to situate the threshold of surplus value extraction—no less than they are in debates over actual wage contracts, and access to welfare and healthcare. The economic route, moreover, is limited by the influence of corporatism within unions—which invites workers to see themselves as existing in partnership with employers, and emphasizes the methods of the guild (such as placing gendered or national restrictions on a defined labor market) over that of organization capable of interrupting a given circuit of capital in order to swing the balance of contracts and that threshold. That corporatist limit, however, inadvertently gives rise to unofficial or wildcat actions and, has increasingly done so, particularly in intra-union conflicts around post-pandemic workplace agreements and economic policy. At the same time, the pandemic has also resulted in new approaches to unionism and industrial action, or combinations around a defense of the most vulnerable workers in a sector—on the understanding that all liquid incomes will tend toward the lowest gravitational points.

This book began by suggesting that exoticist explanations of the pandemic are, ultimately, arguments that seek to externalize liabilities. It proceeded through a discussion of the history of the quarantine as a spatial logic of discipline and providential order, the history of population theory, the political contract and the statistical encoding of borders in understandings of the health and welfare of populations. It then moved into a discussion of the geometries of value—not those imagined by economic nationalism or of a smooth globalization, but of fragile circuits of capital, in which the binding of utility to exchange is far from certain, but in which asymmetric contracts prevail at each step, from extraction to downstream markets. In doing so, it also traced the endogenous turning-points between neoliberalism and authoritarian government, including the switch between a purported rationalism and the intuitive epistemology of charismatic patriarchal authority, the shifting threshold between colonial paternalism and freedom of movement and statistical calculations of a nation's re/productive stock that turns into eugenic evaluations and the idea of "herd immunity." It underscores the slips between policy and policing—including the ways in which Black lives have been evaluated as human stock or fugitive labour and policed accordingly. It does not purport to be an exhaustive account of the pandemic—which, at the time of writing, is still ongoing. It is instead written as a way of suggesting that things did not need to turn out as they have, that lives were reckoned and have mattered according to an apparatus and metrics of value whose assumptions can be made explicit and, finally, that everything can be reckoned otherwise.

VĀG
ABO
NDS

Notes

1. See Angela Mitropoulos, "Bordering Colonial Uncertainty," *Political and Legal Anthropology Review* (October 28, 2017), https://polarjournal.org/ bordering-colonial-uncertainty/.

2. As elsewhere, the epistemological approach in this book is informed by a materialist account of how certain ideas come to rule (from Marx); that notwithstanding the prevailing views of an age, conditioned variations in perspective exist and that perspective matters (standpoint); and, finally, that no map is either complete or should be confused with that which it purports to represent, even as the making of maps transforms, as it were, the very territories they chart (per Gödel, Korzybski, Bachelard). As will become clearer, this is very far from a rejection or suspension of the question of truth. On the contrary, it is a way of forcing an explicit description of the means by which truths are asserted and of clarifying the conditions of statements.

3. For a longer discussion of asymmetry and surplus value, particularly in relation to contracts and the distribution of risk, see Angela Mitropoulos, *Contract & Contagion: From Biopolitics to Oikonomia* (Wivenhoe: Minor Compositions, 2012), pp. 31, 77.

4. R. Taggart Murphy, "East and West: Geocultures and the Coronavirus," *New Left Review*, 121 (2020).

5. While modified over time, the *hukou* is a system of household registration that links welfare entitlements to household and geography,

resulting in a system where internal migrants have fewer entitlements where they work. See also *Chuǎng*, "Left to Rot: The Crisis in China's Pension System," *Chuǎng* (blog), March 2, 2020, http://chuangcn.org/2020/03/left-to-rot/.

6. Angela Mitropoulos, "Archipelago of Risk: Uncertainty, Borders and Migration Detention Systems," *New Formations* 84–85 (2015): pp. 163–83.

7. Jin Wu, et al., "28,000 Missing Deaths: Tracking the True Toll of the Coronavirus Crisis," *New York Times*,www.nytimes.com/interactive/2020/04/21/world/coronavirus-missing-deaths.html (accessed April 23, 2020 [subsequently updated]).

8. "In Shielding Hospitals from COVID-19, Britain Left the Weakest Exposed," *Reuters*, www.reuters.com/investigates/special-report/health-coronavirus-britain-elderly/ (accessed May 7, 2020).

9. Mitropoulos, *Contract & Contagion*, p. 77.

10. Hiroshi Sato, "Housing Inequality and Housing Poverty in Urban China in the Late 1990s," *China Economic Review* 17, no. 1 (January 1, 2006), pp. 37–50.

11. "Social Contagion," *Chuǎng* (blog), February 26, 2020, http://chuangcn.org/2020/02/social-contagion/.

12. Its air quality has had an annual average PM2.5 concentration of over 120µg/m3. For comparison, the World Health Organization stipulates an annual average below 10µg/m3—above which total, cardiopulmonary, and lung cancer mortality has been shown to increase with more than 95 percent confidence. Moreover, while Wuhan's employment-linked private health insurance and the fee-for-service health system established in China since the 1980s has changed and has done so since the pandemic began, it nevertheless continues to represent an enormous shift from the principle of public healthcare to

that of 'personal responsibility' conditioned by private wealth. Michal Krzyzanowski, et al., "Air Pollution in the Mega-Cities," *Current Environmental Health Reports* 1 (September 1, 2014), pp.185–91; Arden Pope, et al., "Lung Cancer, Cardiopulmonary Mortality, and Long-Term Exposure to Fine Particulate Air Pollution," *JAMA* 287, no. 9 (March 6, 2002), pp. 1132–41.

13. Yuanli Liu, "China's Public Health-Care System: Facing the Challenges," *Bulletin of the World Health Organization* 82 (July 2004), pp. 532–38.

14. Pingan Zheng, Thomas Faunce, and Kellie Johnston, "Public Hospitals in China: Privatisation, the Demise of Universal Health Care and the Rise of Patient-Doctor Violence," *Journal of Law and Medicine* 13, no. 4 (2006), p. 465.

15. Ping Liu, et al., "Are Pangolins the Intermediate Host of the 2019 Novel Coronavirus (2019-NCoV)?," *BioRxiv*, February 20, 2020; Xingguang Li, et al., "Evolutionary History, Potential Intermediate Animal Host, and Cross-Species Analyses of SARS-CoV-2," *Journal of Medical Virology* 92, no. 6 (2020): 602–11; Maciej F. Boni, et al., "Evolutionary Origins of the SARS-CoV-2 Sarbecovirus Lineage Responsible for the COVID-19 Pandemic," *BioRxiv*, March 31, 2020, 2020.

16. Mary Douglas, *Purity and Danger: An Analysis of Concepts of Pollution and Taboo* (London: Routledge, 1984), pp. 169–71.

17. Charles Darwin, *On the Origin of Species*, ed. Joseph Carroll (Peterborough: Broadview Press, 2003), p. 172.

18. Lynn Margulis, "Symbiosis and Evolution," *Scientific American* 225, no. 2 (1971), pp. 48–61; Lynn Margulis and René Fester, *Symbiosis as a Source of Evolutionary Innovation: Speciation and Morphogenesis* (MIT Press, 1991); Linda M. Van Blerkom, "Role of Viruses in Human

Evolution," *American Journal of Physical Anthropology* 122, no. S37 (2003), pp. 14–46; Frank P. Ryan, "Review Article Viruses as Symbionts," *Symbiosis*, 2007.

19. Margulis, "Symbiosis and Evolution," p. 49.

20. Gilles Deleuze and Felix Guattari, *A Thousand Plateaus: Capitalism and Schizophrenia*, trans. Brian Massumi (London: Continuum, 2004), p. 12.

21. "Marx to Ferdinand Lassalle," in *Marx and Engels: Collected Works*, vol. 41 (London: Lawrence and Wishart, 2010), pp. 246–47; Marx and Friedrich Engels, *Manifesto of the Communist Party* (Moscow: Progress Press, 1977), p. 21.

22. Karl Marx, "Critique of Hegel's Doctrine of the State," in *Early Writings* (London: Penguin, 1984), p. 175; Karl Marx, *Grundrisse: Foundations for a Critique of Political Economy*, trans. Martin Nicolaus (London: Penguin, 1993), p. 496.

23. Leen Vijgen, et al., "Complete Genomic Sequence of Human Coronavirus OC43: Molecular Clock Analysis Suggests a Relatively Recent Zoonotic Coronavirus Transmission Event," *Journal of Virology* 79, no. 3 (February 2005), pp. 1595–1604.

24. Keith Ansell-Pearson, *Viroid Life: Perspectives on Nietzsche and the Transhuman Condition* (New York: Routledge, 1997), p. 17.

25. Britta L. Jewell and Nicholas P. Jewell, "The Huge Cost of Waiting to Contain the Pandemic," *New York Times*, April 14, 2020.

26. T. Jefferson, et al., "Physical Interventions to Interrupt or Reduce the Spread of Respiratory Viruses," *Cochrane Database of Systematic Reviews*, 6:7, 2011.

27. Angela Mitropoulos, "Against Quarantine," *New Inquiry*, February 13, 2020, https://thenewinquiry.com/against-quarantine/.

28. Michel Foucault, *Security, Territory, Population: Lectures at the Collège de France, 1977–78*,

trans. Graham Burchell (London: Palgrave Macmillan, 2007), p. 10.

29. Michel Foucault, *The Birth of Biopolitics: Lectures at the Collège de France, 1978–1979*, ed. Graham Burchell, trans. Arnold I Davidson (Springer, 2008), pp. 43, 64–65; Mitropoulos, *Contract & Contagion*, pp. 135–37.

30. As will be discussed below, it also forgets the genealogical conditions which Marx alluded to in his critique of Hegel's political corporatism.

31. See Mitropoulos, *Contract & Contagion*.

32. Peta Longhurst, "Quarantine Matters: Colonial Quarantine at North Head, Sydney and Its Material and Ideological Ruins," *International Journal of Historical Archaeology* 20, no. 3 (2016), pp. 589–600.

33. Thalia Anthony, "The Return to the Legal and Citizenship Void: Indigenous Welfare Quarantining in the Northern Territory and Cape York," *Balayi: Culture Law and Colonialism* 10 (2009), p. 29.

34. Shelley Bielefeld, "Compulsory Income Management and Indigenous Australians: Delivering Social Justice or Furthering Colonial Domination," *UNSW Law Journal* 35 (2012), p. 535; Alison Vivian and Ben Schokman, "The Northern Territory Intervention and the Fabrication of 'Special Measures,'" *Australian Indigenous Law Review* 13, no. 1 (2009), pp. 78–106.

35. Heather Gridley, et al., "The Australian Psychological Society and Australia's Indigenous People: A Decade of Action," *Australian Psychologist* 35, no. 2 (July 1, 2000), p. 88.

36. Robert S. Gottfried, *Black Death* (New York: Simon and Schuster, 2010), xvi.

37. Dr. William Schaffner, head of preventive medicine at Vanderbilt University's medical school, in Donald McNeil, "Using a Tactic Unseen in a Century, Countries Cordon Off Ebola-Racked Areas," *New York Times*, August 12, 2014.

38. See Angela Mitropoulos, "Dispensing God's Care," *New Inquiry*, June 12, 2017; Angela Mitropoulos, "Lifeboat Capitalism, Catastrophism, Borders," *Dispatches* 1 (November 2018).

39. *Preventing Teen Pregnancy: Coordinating Community Efforts. Hearing Before the Subcommittee on Human Resources and Intergovernmental Relations* (Washington DC: US Federal Government, 1999), p. 42; Laurie Garrett, "Meet Trump's New, Homophobic Public Health Quack," *Foreign Policy*, March 23, 2018.

40. See Donna Minkowitz, "Why Racists (and Liberals!) Keep Writing for Quillette," *Nation*, December 5, 2019; Sarah Jones, "Will the 2020s Be the Decade of Eugenics?," *Intelligencer*, January 2, 2020.

41. Toby Young, "Cometh the Hour, Cometh the Man: A Profile of Boris Johnson," *Quillette*, July 23, 2019.

42. Jonathan Calvert, et al., "Coronavirus: 38 Days When Britain Sleepwalked into Disaster," *The Times*, April 19, 2020.

43. https://twitter.com/richardhorton1/status/1252183975893884933.

44. Allison Pearson, "We Need You, Boris–Your Health Is the Health of the Nation," *Telegraph*, April 7, 2020,

45. Tim Shipman and Caroline Wheeler, "Coronavirus: Ten Days that Shook Britain," *Sunday Times*, March 22, 2020.

46. Mike Wright, "Calls for Government to Investigate 'Alarming' Number of BAME Deaths in Health Service," *Telegraph*, April 15, 2020; Carole Cadwalladr, "'They Can't Get Away With This': Doctor Who Took Protest to No 10," *Guardian*, April 20, 2020.

47. www.youtube.com/watch?v=2XRc389TvG8.

48. Paul Fine, "Herd Immunity: History, Theory, Practice," *Epidemiologic Reviews* 15:2 (1993), pp. 265–302.

49. Figures from Centre for Evidence-Based Medicine, Oxford University (April 19, 2020).

50. Hobbes is Thucydides's most famous English translator, the Athenian historian and general whose history of the fifth century BC Peloponnesian War is as much about war as the plague that devastated Athens. See Clifford Orwin, "Stasis and Plague: Thucydides on the Dissolution of Society," *Journal of Politics* 50, no. 4 (November 1, 1988), pp. 831–47.

51. Thomas Hobbes, *Leviathan*, ed. Crawford Brough Macpherson (London: Penguin, 1976).

52. Ibid., pp. 127, 223.

53. Thomas Malthus, "A Summary View of the Principle of Population," in *On Population: Three Essays* (New York: New American Library, 1960), p. 26; Thomas Malthus, *An Essay on the Principle of Population* (London: St. Paul's Church, 1798), p. 42.

54. Malthus, "A Summary View of the Principle of Population," p. 14.

55. Boris Johnson, "Global Over-Population is the Real Issue," *Telegraph*, October 25, 2007 (accessed via www.telegraph.co.uk/comment/3643551/Global-over-population-is-the-real-issue.html).

56. John P. Fox, et al., "Herd Immunity: Basic Concept and Relevance to Public Health Immunization Practices," *American Journal of Epidemiology* 94, no. 3 (1971), pp. 179–89.

57. Ibid., p. 179.

58. W.W.C. Topley and G.S. Wilson, "The Spread of Bacterial Infection. The Problem of Herd-Immunity," *Epidemiology & Infection* 21, no. 3 (1923), p. 249.

59. Alain Desrosières, *The Politics of Large Numbers: A History of Statistical Reasoning* (Cambridge: Harvard University Press, 2002); Angela Mitropoulos, "Archipelago of Risk: Uncertainty, Borders and Migration Detention Systems," *New Formations* 84, no. 84–85 (2015), pp. 163–83.

60. For a discussion of this in Aristotle and Marx, see Angela Mitropoulos, "Oikonomia," *Philosophy Today* 63, no. 4 (2019), pp. 1025–36.

61. Louis I. Dublin and Alfred J. Lotka, "On the True Rate of Natural Increase," *Journal of the American Statistical Association* 20, no. 151 (1925), pp. 305–39.

62. Fine, "Herd Immunity," p. 274.

63. Sky News, "UK needs to get COVID-19 for 'herd immunity'," www.youtube.com/watch?v=2XRc389TvG8.

64. Topley and Wilson, "The Spread of Bacterial Infection," p. 249.

65. "Coronavirus Disproportionately Affecting BAME Communities in UK, New Figures Show," *Independent*, April 21, 2020.

66. Karl Marx and Friedrich Engels, *The German Ideology* (New York: International Publishers, 1970), p. 94.

67. Corrado Gini, "The Scientific Basis of Fascism," *Political Science Quarterly* 42, no. 1 (1927), p. 102.

68. For more on Böckh, see Ian Hacking, *The Taming of Chance* (Cambridge: Cambridge University Press, 2002), p. 69.

69. Friedrich Nietzsche, *Beyond Good and Evil, Prelude to a Philosophy of the Future* (New York: Courier Corporation, 2012), pp. 23–31, 69.

70. Per 2017 OECD data on expenditure on retail pharmaceuticals per capita, and 2018 data on total health spending.

71. In Katie Thomas and Denise Grady, "Trump's Embrace of Unproven Drugs to Treat Coronavirus Defies Science," *New York Times*, March 20, 2020; Donald J. Trump, "@realDonaldTrump," *Twitter*, March 22, 2020.

72. Jacques Derrida, "Plato's Pharmacy," in *Dissemination*, ed. Barbara Johnson (Chicago: University of Chicago Press, 1981), pp. 61–171; Plato, *Phaedrus*, ed. Reginald Hackforth (Cambridge: Cambridge University Press, 1972).

73. Plato, *The Republic*, ed. G.R.F. Ferrari, trans. Tom Griffith (Cambridge: Cambridge University Press, 2000), 3.389b–c, 459c.

74. Ibid., 561d–562b; For a longer discussion of Plato's politics and fascist metaphysics, see Angela Mitropoulos, "Art of Life, Art of War: Movement, Un/Common Forms, and Infrastructure," *E-Flux*, no. 90 (April 2018).

75. Didier Raoult, "Un Remède Pour Le Climat?," *Le Point*, October 18, 2016; Catherine Mary, "Sound and Fury in the Microbiology Lab," *Science* 335, no. 6072 (March 2, 2012).

76. Yves Sciama, "Is France's President Fueling the Hype Over an Unproven Coronavirus Treatment?," *Science*, AAAS, April 9, 2020.

77. Philippe Gautret, et al., "Hydroxychloroquine and Azithromycin as a Treatment of COVID-19: Results of an Open-Label Non-Randomized Clinical Trial," *International Journal of Antimicrobial Agents*, March 20, 2020.

78. "Statement on IJAA Paper," International Society of Antimicrobial Chemotherapy, www.isac.world/news-and-publications/official-isac-statement (accessed April 11, 2020).

79. "Clinical and Microbiological Effect of a Combination of Hydroxychloroquine and Azithromycin in 80 COVID-19 Patients with at Least a Six-Day Follow up: An Observational Study," www.mediterranee-infection.com/wp-content/uploads/2020/03/COVID-IHU-2-1.pdf.

80. "Coronavirus : Les Effets Indésirables Graves s'accumulent Sur l'hydroxychloroquine," *Le Monde*. April 9, 2020, www.lemonde.fr/planete/article/2020/04/09/covid-19-les-effets-indesirables-graves-s-accumulent-sur-l-hydroxychloroquine_6036139_3244.html.

81. Kathryn Eastburn, "Texas City COVID-19 Patients Receive Hydroxychloroquine," *Daily News*, accessed April 10, 2020, www.galvnews.com/news/free/article_b59bab46-543a-5116-8e37-2f330a8fc008.html.

82. Michael Rinella, *Pharmakon: Plato, Drug Culture, and Identity in Ancient Athens* (Lexington Books, 2010), p. 74.

83. www.sec.gov/Archives/edgar/data/1682 852/000112760220014877/xslF345X03/ form4.xml.

84. International Monetary Fund, "World Economic Outlook. Chapter 1: The Great Lockdown," April 2020.

85. See Angela Mitropoulos, "Lifeboat Capitalism, Catastrophism, Borders," *Dispatches* 1 (November 2018), http://dispatchesjournal. org/articles/162/.

86. See Angela Mitropoulos and Dick Bryan, "Social Benefit Bonds: Financial Markets Inside the State," in Gabrielle Meagher and Susan Goodwin, eds., *Markets, Rights and Power in Australian Social Policy* (Sydney: Sydney University Press, 2016), pp. 153 –68.

87. "Fact Sheet: Pandemic Emergency Financing Facility," Text/HTML, World Bank, www. worldbank.org/en/topic/pandemics/brief/ fact-sheet-pandemic-emergency-financing- facility (accessed April 12, 2020).

88. Asian Development Bank, "Global Shortage of Personal Protective Equipment amid COVID-19: Supply Chains, Bottlenecks, and Policy Implications," Asian Development Bank Briefs, 130 (April 2020).

89. For a longer discussion of these points, see Mitropoulos, "Art of Life, Art of War."

90. See Mitropoulos, "Art of Life, Art of War."

91. Jonathan Allen, et al., "Silent Partner in Coronavirus Contract Sold Protective Gear to U.S. for Double the Cost." *NBC News*, April 19, 2020.

92. Scott Anderson, "Coronavirus-Related Price Gouging Reported At 16 Wisconsin Stores." *Patch*, March 25, 2020.

93. Luigi Zingales and Roy Shapira, "Is Pollution Value-Maximizing? The DuPont Case"

(United States: National Bureau of Economic Research, 2017).

94. Wendee Nicole, "PFOA and Cancer in a Highly Exposed Community: New Findings from the C8 Science Panel," *Environmental Health Perspectives* 121, no. 11–12 (2013): A340.

95. Sarah Neville and Peter Foster, "How Poor Planning Left the UK without Enough PPE," *Financial Times*, May 1, 2020.

96. Centers for Disease Control and Prevention, "Identifying Critical Infrastructure During COVID-19" (United States, March 18, 2020); Barack Obama, "Presidential Policy Directive: Critical Infrastructure Security and Resilience" (White House, United States, February 12, 2013), PPD-21.

97. Cybersecurity and Infrastructure Security Agency, "Memorandum on Identification of Essential Critical Infrastructure Workers During Covid-19 Response" (United States, March 19, 2020).

98. Robert Gebeloff, et al., "The Striking Racial Divide in How Covid-19 Has Hit Nursing Homes," *New York Times*, May 21, 2020.

99. J. Carlee Purdum, "States Are Putting Prisoners to Work Manufacturing Coronavirus Supplies," *Conversation*, April 21, 2020.

100. The purportedly anarchist versions of this converts economic units into anthropological categories, as with David Graeber's positive citation of Henry Ford's view of money in "The Truth is out: Money is Just an IOU, and the Banks are Rolling in it," *Guardian*, March 18, 2014.

101. Daniel Alpert, "We Are All Modern Monetarists Now," *Business Insider*, March 23, 2020.

102. Phillip Inman, "The Huge Coronavirus Bailouts Will Need to Be Paid Back. Or Will They?," *Guardian*, March 28, 2020. Moreover, aside from its antecedents in Polanyian economics, modern monetarism draws on human capital theory but mostly, in practice,

on indices of inflation based on the price of mortgages (rather than, say, the price of food and non-commercial rents).

103. The International Labor Organization estimated that, prior to 2020, just over 60 percent of the global workforce was engaged in "informal" employment.

104. Michal Kalecki's theory of the causes of unemployment in the 1930s, based on a categorical distinction between employment and unemployment, holds that capital prefers the threat of unemployment as a means of ensuring political and workplace stability and in the absence of a direct means of forced labor. Michal Kalecki, "Political Aspects of Full Employment" *Political Quarterly* 14, no. 4 (1943), pp. 322–30. See also Angela Mitropoulos, "Encoding the Law of the Household and the Standardisation of Uncertainty," in *Mapping Precariousness, Labour Insecurity and Uncertain Livelihoods: Subjectivities and Resistance*, ed. Emiliana Armano, Arianna Bove, and Annalisa Murgia (London: Routledge, 2017), p. 214.

Thanks to our Patreon Subscribers:

Abdul Alkalimat
Andrew Perry

Who have shown their generosity and comradeship in difficult times.